You Always Have Options℠

Guiding Principles for Managing Money

Derek E. Johnson

unique
PUBLISHERS

Tanya,
May you experience all the desires
of your heart and enjoy every minute!
Wherever this road leads you, remember,
You Always Have Options!
—Derek Johnson

You Always Have Options^{SM}: Guiding Principles for Managing Money

ISBN 0-9786197-0-6

The editing supervisor is Jennifer Johnson of J. Johnson Consulting, jjohnsonconsulting.com.

Cover design provided by Alexander Hickman of DeMarco Suade Studios, suadegraphx@bellsouth.net.

Books from Unique Publishers are available with volume discounts for organizations. To purchase additional books, contact the Director of Sales, at sales@uniquepublishers.com, or visit **uniquepublishers.com**.

To discuss and discover additional options, join the community at **youalwayshaveoptions.com**.

Acknowledgements

I dedicate this book to my children, Xavier and Morgan, and to their generation. I expect them to be the most empowered and financially proficient people in history. I thank my wife, Jennifer, for her patience, support, wisdom, perspective. You name it... she gives it to me. To my parents, thanks for showing me the value of hard work and the joy of helping others achieve their goals. To all my family and friends, you are my silent inspiration. I especially thank those who have sacrificed to make sure that I was able to pursue my dreams. Every kind word and every dollar made a difference. In my heart, I know that Delinda Brown Clark, Daniel Waggoner, Carl & Frankie Robinson, and Richard Hall are watching me from heaven and know that a large part of who I am is because of who they were. Finally, thank you to everyone who ever tried to teach me that each decision you make should give you more options. Each dollar you make should enable you to make even more money and open new doors. I finally get it...

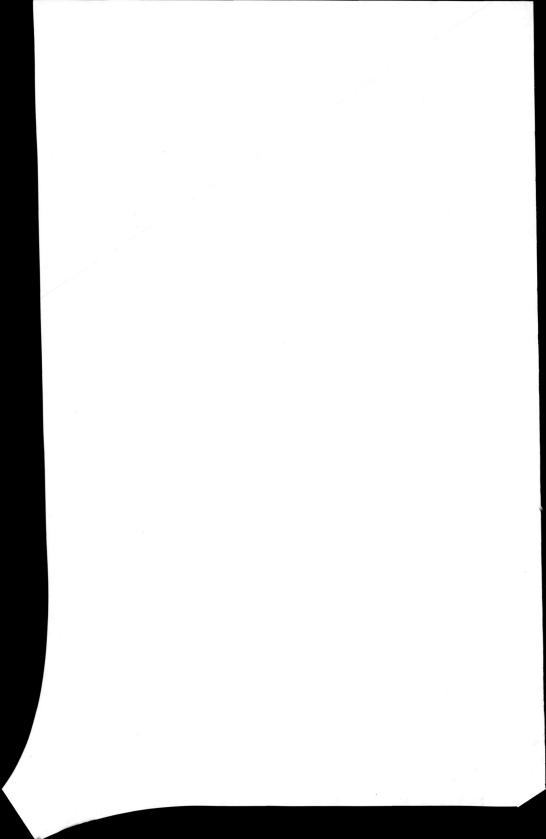

Table of Contents

Introduction

The *You Always Have Options*^{SM} series will assist anyone who wants to maximize their talents and resources to improve their quality of life. By laying out Guiding Principles for some of life's most important areas, these books can serve as a reference to ensure that future generations have the knowledge necessary to control their own destiny. With each topic, my hope is that fear and lack of information will no longer have the ability to isolate those who want the best out of life.

When it comes to money, what you don't know will inevitably cost you. This book is for all of you who believe there has to be a better way. By discussing many of the underlying financial concepts that may or may not be taught in classrooms, there is no doubt you will become more empowered to make, manage, and spend money in the most effective manner possible.

These next few pages will start you on a journey that will expand the ways you look at making, saving, and spending money. The Guiding Principles (each represents a chapter) found in this book are concepts that empower you as a member of the global economy. Whether you have yet to make your first dollar, or you are sitting on so much money that you do not know how to spend it, your future will be more stable financially if you can internalize the material before you. The days of leaving your financial future in the hands of others are over. You can and should control your own financial future.

If you are still a student, think of school as your first job. If you treat it as such, you will be more focused in school. Every failing grade is like a demotion or a pay cut. Each "A" is like a pay raise. The grades you make in school will have a strong correlation with the types of jobs you will be able to get in the future. Focus less on how much money you might make, and more on what you will do with the money you make. Consider how you can use your money to make more money. What will it take to make you financially independent? How can you use money to increase your earning potential? With every choice, you should consider whether you are opening more doors or taking a path that will restrict your freedom.

If the material in this book is already clear to you, find a way to teach others what you know. Pass this book to someone who needs it. Teach the principles to your children. Make it a goal to learn and teach more advanced concepts than are covered in this book. It takes time and creativity to increase financial awareness and competence. I hope you will be inspired to write your own books, design computer software, and create games that help all of us become smarter about managing money.

My only request as you read this book is that you take some action. Find at least one Guiding Principle that you can master and over time fill up your treasure chest. There are blank pages at the end of the book for you to write down any personal thoughts that you have while reading. This book has little value if it is only inspirational and makes you feel better. Ultimately, you have to live better, so let's get started.

Opportunity

On your journey, there will be times when opportunities are hard to find, it is then when you must create your own...

Guiding Principle 1
Earn More and Spend Less

However simple this may sound, financial success boils down to making more money than you spend. The ability to keep your expenses below your income is the main difference between people who live comfortably and those who fall into financial hardship. Ultimately, you should not define success by how much money you make, but by how much you keep.

There are only two ways to master this Guiding Principle. Either make more money or spend less for the things you buy. Neither is easy, but both can be within your control.

You can increase how much money you make in many ways, some of which you can do simultaneously. Mastery of this principle begins when you learn to use one method of making money to finance other more profitable ways of making money. In the beginning, it may take tremendous effort, but as you become more successful, you can leverage your experiences to open new doors. Listed below are a few ways to increase your earning potential.

♦ **Education** – College is not the only option. Continuing education classes, seminars, the internet, magazine subscriptions, and the library all offer ways to increase your knowledge base. Evaluate each option as a tool to make you more talented in your craft. Choose an educational path that makes sense to you as an investment. The education by itself has little value if you cannot use it to help you achieve something else. Each degree you get should open new doors for you, in turn, helping you make more money.

♦ **Entrepreneurship** – Consider selling goods or services as an independent businessperson. You can do anything from cutting grass, catering, or tax preparation. These jobs enable you to make money on your own terms even while you maintain your primary job.

3

◆ **Working a second job** – Choose second jobs (bartending, direct sales, real estate agent) that are performance-based (tips or commission) to keep you motivated when working the extra hours.

◆ **Promotions** – Promotions are not always in your control, but do not feel that you ever owe someone for giving you a promotion. Earn your promotions; do not wait for someone to hand them to you. Understand the difference between you and the people ahead of you, and strive to do the things that you can control to make yourself eligible for a promotion.

◆ **Interest-bearing accounts** – Banks and credit unions offer accounts that pay you just for keeping your money with them. Several firms offer interest bearing checking and savings accounts. If you have money that you are saving toward larger purchases, be sure to keep this money in an account that pays you as much interest as possible.

◆ **Rental property** – If you can afford to buy a second property, find one for which you can afford the mortgage, taxes, and maintenance expenses. Be sure that the amount of rent you can charge allows you to make a profit each month. Any equity you can gain on the property is a bonus, but be sure you are making money month to month. If you are not able to hold the property long enough to see significant appreciation in the value of the house, consider selling the house by yourself or through a for sale by owner company. Agent commissions can significantly cut into any profit you could have made.

◆ **Stocks & Bonds** – You can buy stocks of companies that are undervalued or growing and sell when they appreciate. Investing in stocks can be risky, so invest time in education before investing by yourself. Even if you don't have the confidence or time to learn how to invest by yourself, you can grow your money in financial markets by investing with trustworthy and successful financial firms.

Reducing how much you spend may actually be more effective than increasing how much you make. For the most part, controlling expenses is more about discipline and patience than it is any secret tricks. Some quick ways to cut expenses include:

♦ **Buying in large quantities** – Learn how companies set prices. When shopping for groceries, notice that the containers for items like water cost the manufacturer more than the content in the bottle. Therefore, you actually get a discount when you buy larger quantities. That is why shopping at wholesale clubs can save you an extra 10% to 20% on most items. It is cheaper to sell a 30-pack of water from one store than to break up that pack of 30 bottles of water into five 6-packs to sell at five different stores. The vendor will gladly give you a small discount to get you to buy the 30-pack.

Many grocery store items now also show the "per unit" price. A 24-ounce box of cereal costs more than a 16-ounce box, but the per unit cost of the 24-ounce box is less. If you buy cereal on a regular basis, it is in your best interest to buy the bigger box. You will pay more now, but over time you will save money. Whenever possible buy items where the "per unit" price is lower.

♦ **Being "fashionably late" (literally)** – Timing is a primary driver for many products like clothing and electronics. I'm not going to cross the line here and advocate everyone stop buying the latest fashions or gadgets. However, I challenge you to study the pricing trends. Know how long it takes your favorite retailer to move an item to the sale rack. All retailers have to do it because they do not want the inflow of new clothes to outpace the outflow of old. Develop relationships with the people you buy from and let them know you understand how you help each other. Merchants who have a relationship with you will do more to maintain that bond. You are an equal partner in any transaction, so enter each sale as a businessperson.

♦ **Think long-term** - When making large purchases, think about the total bill, not just the month-to-month expense. Consider if you purchase a $200,000 house on a 30-year loan at 7%. In 30 years, you will have paid $479.017.80. That is almost $280,000 extra in interest. The same house with a 15 year mortgage will cost a total of $323,578.18, saving you over $150,000 overall. Yes, the month-to-month payment may be higher, but think overall cost whenever possible. The same math applies to buying a car. Be cautious of deals that extend the length of the loan period to help you afford the monthly bill. If the monthly payment is the largest concern, try to find a way to increase your down payment by saving more money before buying the car. The benefit is that you do not pay the extra interest associated with longer-term loans.

♦ **Get some help** – If you are single, get a roommate or two if you can handle the social aspects of sharing space. Living expenses can place the most constraints on your ability to control spending, but having roommates to split rent and utilities can help you get a jumpstart on your financial future. Pick roommates with something to lose. In other words, you want the kind of person who worries about paying the bills on time. Find people who value having good credit and a good reputation. Team up with people who have long-term goals and are actively pursuing them.

Another option is to live at home with your parents for a little longer after high school or college. You do not want to be a freeloader once you start working, so contribute your fair share to the household expenses. Just a couple of years at home when you are working full time can give you a tremendous jump on building the savings you will need for investing and purchasing a home.

♦ **Spend your money with those who spend their money with you** - A community is more than a group of people who live close to each other. In a financial sense, people and businesses rely on each other for their mutual existence and growth. You may cut a neighbors yard for a month in exchange for tax advice. Use your creativity. Make sure the barber/hairdresser you visit each week knows what you do for a living and what you can do for them. If you can cook, bringing in an extra plate when you come to get your haircut could get you a free haircut one day. Find ways to recycle money with those that have an interest in seeing you do well.

♦ **Accept invitations to save** – Manufacturers and stores offer several ways for the customer to save money. These options include coupons, rebates, and seasonal sales. You are always in a position to decline the invitation if you are not interested. Simply put, manufacturers distribute coupons hoping to attract new customers. When you see a coupon for a product you regularly purchase, use it! It may be a nuisance, but saving $10 or more per week (over $500 a year) on groceries can add up when you are reducing expenses. Nobody likes the idea of paying for a dinner date with a coupon. However, you can always order two meals and use one for dinner and the other for lunch the next day. Do what works for you. The bottom line is to avoid spending money that you do not have to spend. Balance pride and creativity to save money.

♦ **Get comfortable thinking fast** – In the money game, it often boils down to thinking in percentages. Budgeting is necessary, but sometimes we get overwhelmed in the details and create budgets that we cannot follow. Do not build your budget based on your total gross income. Instead, you have to look at the amount you actually bring home. Analyze what you spend on rent/mortgages, food, utilities, entertainment, and clothing. When you add up all your expenses and savings, the total should be 100% of the income you bring home. One hundred percent is all you can spend, even if you have all the credit in the world. Also, avoid budgeting based on what you expect to get from bonuses, tax returns, or credit. If you overspend in one area, you have to cut back in another. If you pay a late fee or make a purchase with a credit card, you are breaking your budget and you should sacrifice something of equal value. Similarly, if you are able to save a few percent by buying tax-deductible items or purchasing items when retailers offer promotions, you can increase the savings portion of your budget.

Principle in Action:

1. Identify and rank three methods for how you can increase the amount of money you make.

2. Identify and rank three methods for decreasing your monthly expenses or long-term expenses.

Guiding Principle 2
Search for the Hidden Costs

For your own sanity and financial stability, look beyond the listed price to make sure you know the total cost of the major purchases in life. In many situations, you may not be able to afford things that you initially thought were in reach. For many larger purchases, you are actually buying the right to spend more money. If you are aware of the potential follow up costs, your definition of what you can afford may change or you may just delay your purchase until you can actually afford everything involved.

New House – Let's take a house that costs $100,000. Assume a 30 year mortgage at 8% APR. State and local property taxes will be approximately 1% of the house value each year. Assume you have 10% for the down payment. As a homeowner, you will have different ways of deferring or avoiding some of the items listed below. The goal of listing them is not to scare you, but rather to prepare you so that you do not walk away from the first months of home ownership hard-pressed to buy food.

1. **Mortgage** –The mortgage is how much you will pay the bank for the ability to spread the cost of the house over 10, 15, or 30 years. In the first few years, the majority of your mortgage payment will go toward interest. For our example house, the 30-year mortgage monthly payment is $660 a month. Of that first month's payment, only $60 actually goes toward paying down the $100,000 house (with $10,000 down you are financing $90,000). The remaining $600 is interest that the bank collects for financing your loan. The interest is tax deductible, meaning it will help reduce your overall tax bill. However, in general, most of the interest paid is lost money. Traditional mortgages have a fixed interest rate for the term of the loan. Sometimes it makes sense to get an Adjustable Rate Mortgage (ARM), which has a fixed rate for a few years, then the rate changes as a function of the long-term treasury rates. ARMs are favorable when interest rates are decreasing because your mortgage will decrease over time. Also remember, the shorter the term

of the loan, the lower the interest rate. Although, the monthly amount is higher on short-term loans, you pay less over the life of the loan.

2. **PMI** – Private Mortgage Insurance – If you are unable to place 20% as a down payment on your home, you can finance the rest, but you'll pay PMI until you have 20% equity in the home (i.e. until you've paid enough principle to have 20% of the house paid for). For our sample mortgage, PMI is approximately **$70**/month. One option for minimizing the impact of PMI is to prepay the PMI fees and have them added to your mortgage.

When interest rates are low, it sometimes makes sense to use a Line of Credit option to finance the amount between your down payment and the 20% value of the home. Doing so can eliminate PMI. In this case, if you put down $10,000, you would get a Line of Credit for $10,000. A Line of Credit works just like a credit card. You can pay just interest or you can pay down the balance on the Line of Credit at your own pace. Typically, you have 10 years to pay off the line of credit balance. If you pay off the balance early, you will have the ability to use the Line of Credit account as an additional credit line that you can access whenever you choose. You are almost guaranteed that the interest rate will always be lower than any credit card. Since interest rates can always go up, aggressively pay down the balance on your line of credit account to keep the payments under control.

3. **Mortgage Prepay** – Depending on what day of the month you go to closing to purchase the house, you will be required to prepay the remaining days of the month's mortgage. For this example, we are smart and planned our closing date for the end of the month. **$0**

4. **Home Inspection** – Just prior to closing, you should hire a home inspector to make sure that everything in the home is up to an acceptable standard. There are things that you would never know to look for, so don't just trust your eyes or the builder's word. Hire a professional. **$200**

5. **Taxes** – Property taxes vary based on where you live. Bear in mind, taxes may go up as the tax rate changes or if the home is appraised at a higher value. **$1,000**

6. **Insurance** – Property insurance covers the interior and exterior of the home in the event of damage. The cost of insurance is a function of your deductible. The deductible is the amount you have to pay when you file a claim. The higher the deductible, the lower your monthly payment will be. Let's use **$500** a year as a cost for insurance on this home.

7. **Appliances** – If you have made the move from an apartment or dorm, you do not have any appliances to bring to your new home. A refrigerator is necessary and costs around **$500**. Most people also buy a washer and dryer, adding another **$500** for a total of **$1000**.

8. **Window Treatments** – Probably the most often overlooked expense in a new home are curtains and blinds. If you pay someone to do it for you, the expense can quickly rise to over $1000. However, if you are the do it yourself type, you can buy blinds and curtains and hang them yourself. They may lack the professional touch, but you can keep the cost in the hundreds instead of the thousands. For this example, let's use **$200**.

9. **Lawn Care** – You will have to buy your own lawn mower, rake, blower, hedge clippers, and garden hoses or pay a service to take care of your yard work. Let's assume we buy our own equipment, add another **$300**.

10. **Deposits to turn on utilities** – If you are new to paying bills or are moving to a different part of town, it is highly probable that you will pay additional deposits to get gas, water, sewer, garbage collection, electricity, phone, and cable turned on in your name. Notice, things like garbage collection, water, and sewer were hidden in your rent payment. **$200**

11. **Furniture** – One of the main reasons people move from an apartment to a house is for more space. When you first move, the temptation is to try to fill each room with furniture, or replace old furniture. Resist the

temptation if at all possible. You will be under a fair amount of stress from closing and moving, so let's assume we move in with just what we already own. **$0**

12. **Moving Expenses** – If you have any existing furniture at all, you will likely have to rent a truck to move it. We will assume you are doing it with some friends that you feed that day, instead of paying for a moving service. **$100**

13. **Increased gasoline expenses per month** – Oftentimes, many of us choose to move to communities that are not close to our jobs. This can easily add an additional **$50 to $100** a month in Gasoline expenses.

As much as possible, defer the costs that you can, so that you don't have to start loading up your credit cards as soon as you move into your new home. Even if you can qualify for a home loan today, be sure that you have the extra money you will need for down payments, closing costs, and unavoidable start up costs. For the scenario above, even after paying your down payment and closing costs, you could still spend over **$3600** to make your home livable.

New Car – Assume the car price is $20,000, financed over 5 years with an 8% interest rate. Assume the state tax is 5%. Expect to put down a 10% down payment. Assume you drive 12,000 miles a year.

1. **Monthly Payment** – Assuming that you paid off the sales tax of $1000 and put the 10% down, you have knocked $2000 off the principle. Therefore, you are financing $18,000 over 5 years with an 8% interest rate - **$365/month** or **$4380/year.**

2. **Insurance** – We will assume you are under 25 (higher insurance bracket), with no previous problems on your record, and you purchase full comprehensive insurance. As with home insurance, you can control your total bill by adjusting the deductible. Some say, the closer you are to paying off the car, the higher the deductible should be. The logic here is that you no longer owe anyone for the value of the vehicle. Also, you

would be less likely to file a claim on a car that is paid off but has depreciated significantly in value. Multiple claims will ultimately result in higher insurance premiums. Typically, you do not want to file claims unless there are few other options, since each claim can raise your insurance premiums. **$100/month** or **$1200/year**

3. **Gas** – The monthly cost of gas is a function of the current prices. When buying a car, consider whether your car will require premium gasoline or regular. On a 15-gallon tank, having to fill up with a higher-grade gasoline can increase your costs by over $3 per fill up. Also, pay attention to the advertised miles per gallon (MPG) your car gets. Higher MPG means fewer trips to the gas station. Let's assume gas is $3 per gallon and you only fill up once a week, the weekly fill up is $45/week, **$180/month** or **$2160/year.**

4. **Maintenance** -
    a. Oil Changes – Oil changes are required every 3 months, average **$25/oil change or $100/year.**
    b. Tire Rotations/Balancing/Replacement – Rotations are recommended every other oil change, while balancing occurs once a year. Tire life fluctuates, but let's assume 50,000 miles for this car. So initially, you spend **$100/year** for balancing and rotations, and an additional **$300 every 4 years** for new tires.
    c. Brakes – Brake life is a function of the type of car (weight) and the way you drive. Brakes need repair or replacement every 2 years. **$200 every two years**
    d. Radiator Flush, Transmission Flushes, Oil Injector Cleanings, etc – The other maintenance charges you will incur can grow quickly, but if you can afford the scheduled maintenance, you can usually avoid much more expensive problems down the road.
    e. Miscellaneous expenses – These include car washes, accessories, and tags/registration. Assume you will spend at least **$500/year** on such items.

Using the numbers above, a car that you buy because the monthly payment is low can cost you much more than you imagined. The total yearly car-related expenses will be approximately **$8500/year** or **$711/month**. As you purchase higher priced cars, the associated costs of automobile ownership will also increase. As you consider how much car you can afford, do your own analysis of the supplemental costs.

5. **Lease vs. Purchase** - One question many have is whether it is better to buy or lease a new car. The answer really is not the same for everybody or every car. The key in making the right decision is in asking and answering the right questions. Leasing by definition just means that you are buying the right to use a vehicle for a set amount of time. When that time is completed, you will owe nothing if you followed the rules of the lease. However, you will own nothing. Buying a car means, you are committing to pay the full value of the car and have the right to own it. If your goals are primarily short term, leasing is a better decision. It allows you to have lower monthly payments, less concern for long-term maintenance, and gives you the ability to change cars every couple of years. If your goals lean more in the direction of long-term value, you should buy. Over time, buying and maintaining a good car will be cheaper than leasing. Also, buying gives you the freedom to drive as much as you want each year (leases charge extra for heavy driving) and the ability to customize your car. For some, the motivation to buy a car just boils down to the pride of ownership and knowing there will be a day when you will have no monthly car payments.

If you choose to lease, use the money you are saving from the reduced monthly payments to make more money or reduce other interest bearing bills. If your lease payment would be $250/month for 3 years, but the purchase price would have been $400/month, use the extra $150/month strategically. You can place that money directly into savings or into stocks or mutual funds. If you have high interest credit card debt, using the extra money saved to pay down the credit card debt is an excellent use of your money. Before you make the decision to buy or lease, make a commitment to line up your decision with your priorities. For example, if you begin leasing, then decide you want to keep the car, you will pay more to buy the car at the end of the lease than you would have if you purchased the car from the beginning. Similarly, if you buy a car, but after two years decide you want a different car, you will have lost significant value. Leasing would have been the smarter financial decision.

College – Understanding the cost of a college education can be confusing. College costs are usually broken down into Tuition, Room & Board, Books, and other miscellaneous fees. In many careers, you will likely need to attend graduate school, so you will want to be careful to keep the costs of your undergraduate program as low as possible.

1. **Tuition** – Typically, tuition will account for the majority of the cost of college. Private colleges and universities charge the same rate for students who live in the same state as the school and for students who live out-of-state. Public schools are able to offer in-state students significantly lower tuition costs than out-of-state students. Sometimes the difference can be higher than 50%. To qualify as an in-state student, you usually have to have established legal residency for a year before you enroll in the school (showing you or your legal guardian has lived in that state for the year before you enroll in school).

    Tuition costs are charged per semester (Spring, Summer, Fall), per quarter (Spring, Summer, Fall, Winter), or per hour (credit). To be a full-time student, you must have at least 12 hours of classes. In most schools using semesters, the tuition cost per term is the same whether you take 12 hours or up to 18 hours. The more hours you take, the sooner you can graduate, but the level of difficulty of your college experience will also increase. The vast majority of financial aid programs are only available to full-time students. In addition, most degree programs assume that you will take an average of 15 hours per term to graduate on time. Make sure you plan the appropriate number of hours to meet all your requirements. A credit hour is the unit schools use to place value on a particular course. A one-hour course meets one hour a week, and gives you one hour (or credit) towards graduation. If you take four

3-hour courses in a semester and pass all of them, you will have 12 hours towards graduation.

2. **Room & Board** – Room and board is how much it costs to provide you a place to sleep and food to eat. If you choose to live in housing provided by the school, you will have to pay their predetermined room and board costs. If you live off-campus in an apartment or house, you are in more control of your expenses and could potentially save a lot of money. Many students will stay on campus for at least their first year or two to help transition them from living at home to living on their own. On-campus students worry less about monthly rent, utilities, or maintenance, since they pay a single fee for all living expenses. Students who live off campus must manage the stresses of property management along with their schoolwork. One option to consider for off-campus living is for a parent to buy a house close to campus that the student can use. The house has potential for additional rental income from other students also, and it will inevitably appreciate during the years the student is in school.

3. **Books** – For most college freshmen, books can be surprisingly expensive, with many books at prices over $100. Students can easily spend $500/semester. One way to manage the costs of books is to buy used books. The supply of used books at the school will disappear quickly. However, you can sometimes find the book online or at local bookstores. Try not to buy too far in advance because some classes change textbooks frequently. Another option is to borrow books from upperclassman or other peers. Many students never sell their books and may be willing to let you use their books during the semester you take the class. For classes in your primary area of study, it is best to buy the book, if possible. Books are not usually covered by federal loans and grants, but small private scholarships are ideal to help pay for books.

4. **Fees** – Most schools offer many services that increase the potential cost of attending school. These fees include facilities fees (labs, gym, clinic, and safety), parking fees, and club/fraternity memberships. These fees are not the most important of your obligations during your collegiate

experience, but they can make a difference in your ability to have balance while in college. As you budget for school, try to make some room for such fees. Federal Aid programs will only pay for fees that are absolutely required by the school. For example, you cannot use your Stafford Loan to pay for a parking pass.

Principle in Action:

1. Find your dream house or dream car and price how much it would cost you in the first year and over the total life of the purchase.

2. Look for ways you can reduce the overall cost of major purchases like homes and cars.

3. Outline the total expected cost for at least three schools that you would like to consider attending.

Planning
No matter how overwhelming the goal, you can achieve it when you create and execute a plan that you believe in.

Guiding Principle 3
Make Decisions to Impact Tomorrow, NOW

The best plans in the world do not amount to much without the first step. You cannot be a millionaire without that first dollar. You cannot be debt free without paying off that first credit card. With any goal you set for yourself, establish clear short-term steps you can take to reach those goals. If you want to retire at 50, how much money do you need saved at 40, at 30, by next year? Procrastination hurts the most when it comes to issues of money because every lost day usually costs you one way or another. There are several ways to take advantage of time.

♦ **Time empowers interest.** Because of the direct correlation between interest and time, time can be as good for you as it is bad. When you are borrowing money, the longer you take to pay off debt, the more unnecessary interest you will pay. Any time you incur a debt, evaluate how much it will cost you when you have finished the payment plan. Make your decisions about whether or not you can afford something based on the total cost of the purchase including interest. If you buy clothes because they are on sale, but you put them on a credit card with a 19% APR, each month you take to pay off the debt eats into the discount you thought you were getting.

♦ **Pay off the lowest balances first.** Instead of maintaining four credit card balances and paying a little above the minimum on each, aggressively payoff the lowest balance. Use the saved money to pay off the balance on the next lowest. You can follow this simple method of debt reduction to regain control of your debt situation. As you pay off the balances, keep the credit card account open. Closing a credit account can actually lower your credit rating. As you reduce your overall debt, call the remaining creditors to see if you qualify for improved finance rates, as your credit score gradually increases.

♦ **Be the first to market**. If you have a business that provides a product or service, try to be first to market. If you have a service or product you can offer, being the first can result in making extra money before competition enters and sets ceilings on how much money you can make. Raising prices is always more difficult than lowering prices when you are in business. New products often have the luxury of defining their own value, so do not waste time and let someone else beat you to the market.

♦ **Create a sense of urgency**. Offer limited time opportunities when selling a product. Making a customer feel as if a particular moment in time is special gives you a greater chance to close a sale. Retail stores make money with never-ending sales. As a customer, you are enticed to buy because you do not want to miss the sale. However, the business cycle of the shop anticipates having to sell some items at a discounted price. Whether you sell 100 shirts at $20, or 200 shirts at a 50% sale price of $10, they still make $2000. All customers are important. Customers who only buy sale items are just as important as those who rush to buy the latest products.

♦ **Buy before things get hot**. Treasures are usually not as valuable when they are new. Many of the wealthiest people are those who where willing to buy when no one else was interested. They are the people who understand the cyclical nature of any economy. For example, a commercial or residential real-estate boom is followed by a slow period. Making money often boils down to buying during the slowest times, not when things are obviously growing. Such investments usually take more patience than money. Do you have the patience to finance and renovate an old abandoned restaurant or car wash in an attractive part of town? Although the business may not make you rich, commercial real estate can increase in value rapidly when a particular part of town starts to become attractive for businesses or new residential projects.

♦ **Minimize how many purchases you finance over time.** When do you really get the emotional satisfaction for a purchase? Is it when you first receive the item, or when you have fully paid for it? Many retailers capitalize on the average buyer's need to have what they want right now, even if it takes 3 to 5 years to pay for it. They will offer you deferred payment or low monthly payments, just to give you the immediate emotional reward of saying "I got it!" I argue that you really "don't have it!" If for some reason, you are not able to make your monthly payments, the lender will repossess the item(s). Part of the challenge with such buying is that there is an unspoken assumption that you will not make any additional purchases that will affect your ability to payoff the initial purchase on time. Credit card companies succeed because the average person never really catches up with their debt. There usually is another way to buy the things you need, so be resourceful and patient.

♦ **Avoid or minimize any unnecessary fees.** If possible, never pay late fees; pay part of a bill if that is all you have and call the person you owe to negotiate different terms. If you have to be late one month, be smart about how you manage the corresponding late fees. Some bills have a set late fee that is not a function of how much you owe. However, bills that have an interest rate component are a double threat. You can be charged a set late fee in addition to being charged extra interest for the time beyond the original due date. If you are late on a credit card bill, the lender will charge a late fee, and you will be responsible for the additional interest due for not paying your previous bill on time. Do not let bad timing cost you unnecessarily. If financial times get so bad that you have to choose which bills to pay first, pay the bill with the greatest penalty for late payments, first.

When you invest in a mutual fund, IRA, or similar investment option, pursue the low or no cost options. Competition has forced financial institutions to make the cost of investing very affordable for most people. You should never feel pressured to take the first option you see. You are the customer, so find the best product for your money.

Principle in Action:

1. Find two ways to make your money make more money (open a savings account, a brokerage account, subscribe to a business magazine).

2. Identify a product or service that you believe will have a lot of growth potential and find a way to invest in it or provide the service yourself.

Guiding Principle 4
Love Inevitably Has a Cost

You may have heard the saying "Love don't cost a thing." In theory, it may be correct; you can give and receive love without ever spending any money. However, in the practical world, maintaining relationships with people you love will have a cost. Some relationships with parents and siblings may require you to assist them when they cannot take care of themselves. The relationships that you choose once you become an adult will undoubtedly have the largest impact on your financial health. For some, marriage instantly increases the income brought into the family and decreases the expenses. The ability to live under one roof and share grocery and utility bills should quickly reduce the overall money coming out of the house. For others, marriage actually increases the burden if the person you are marrying does not work. One of the primary reasons relationships fail is money, so don't be naïve about the financial impact money will have on your relationships and vice-versa. The ability to shift or manage priorities as your relationships evolve is essential to maintaining your financial bearings.

Manage the cost of dating – If you are dating, try to make room for your dating activities in your budget. The tendency when dating is to be very spontaneous, which usually means spend now and worry about how to pay for it later. The art of being spontaneous financially is leaving room in your budget for those types of decisions. For example, you may have $300 each month that you reserve for unplanned entertainment expenses. When you don't use it, that money grows. In four months, you will have $1200 to do something special with the one you are dating. Simple things like this can take some of the financial stress out of dating.

Know as much about your partner's finances as you do your own. When in love, it is tempting to ignore many things about your partner because the emotions of being in love are so high. However, since money is one of the primary reasons that relationships fail, it is worth your time and energy to understand where each partner is financially before joining assets and debt.

If either of you has any serious debt problems, try to get to the root of the problem. Evaluate each other's plan for getting out of debt. Create hypothetical financial plans together. How will you eliminate debt? How will you fund retirement? Could you afford to live together on one income? Try to understand how your partner thinks about money.

Plan budgets with your partner – A budget has no value if both sides do not buy into it. Even if only one of you manages the money, get together to draft the budget. If you incorporate both of your ideas from the beginning, there will be less arguing in the end. Budgets also tell a story about a family's priorities, so conversations about budgets should be family discussions.

Consider the cost of supporting CHILDREN – With the cost of living in most places being so high, both partners typically have to work. This means, you will be spending significant money on childcare. Having children also can directly affect your career options. If you both have jobs that involve significant travel, one of you may have to change jobs. Working extremely late hours can also have an impact on the time you have to spend with your spouse and children, creating more stress. You may have to move out of your one bedroom studio apartment to a house with the extra room you need for the children. Diapers, formula, and baby food will have an impact on your monthly expenses too. As much as possible, financially prepare for children before you start having them. Before you try to have children, set aside money in your budget that will eventually go to new expenses incurred with the arrival of the baby. Having children can be the best thing to happen to you, but if they cause financial strain, you may not realize the blessing you have.

Principle in Action:

1. Prepare a couple of potential budgets that includes the costs involved in having a family. In one scenario, assume that only one partner is working.

2. Estimate the costs of taking care of your parents if they are unable to work and/or exhaust their retirement savings.

Guiding Principle 5
Let the Big Picture Determine Each Small Step

The big picture refers to what matters the most to you. It could be completely about your personal goals or establishing a solid base for the generations that will follow you. The key is to decide what underlying motives will guide your financial decisions. When you have to make difficult decisions about what to do with the money you make, always go back to the big picture.

Make financial goals that outlive you. When it comes to money, the best goals to set are those that continue to grow, possibly even after you are no longer living. The beauty of such goals is that, even if you do not reach your ultimate goal, you will have something to show for your effort. If you need to have $200,000 to retire, consider making your retirement goal $250,000. Upon retirement, you can use the extra $50,000 to help meet unexpected expenses or to be given to your children and grandchildren to give them a head start on their financial journeys.

Long before you retire, consider what you have that you can leave to others. You can do this formally through a living will, but I also recommend doing it informally every few years just to keep the future fresh on your mind. Learning to prioritize is possibly the hardest part of financial planning. No one can do that for you, but you. It is an exercise you should do often, as things change in your life (marriage, children, jobs, etc). Ultimately, you should discipline yourself to have your financial behavior line up with your priorities.

Schedule your down periods. Periods where you have to spend more than normal are unavoidable. To offset such moments, schedule times where you spend less than normal. Even if your income is steady, plan periods of deep spending cuts when times are good and pad your savings. If you tend to spend too much during the holidays, plan a period where you drastically reduce your spending or increase your income. You may cut out all dining-out for two months, carpool, or use public transportation. The method you choose is up to you. The other option is to take a second job or provide a service (lawn care, run errands, cook, etc) to make some extra money that you will not spend until the next holiday season. Begin to manage your finances as a long-term project, instead of as one crisis at a time.

Build and protect your credit to serve as a buffer. The negative and positive consequences of your credit choices last for several years. In its purest sense, credit should be leveraged to help you make more money. In the event of extreme problems, credit is useful to provide you some time to regain your footing until you can stabilize your finances. In order for credit to be available as a safety net, you have to avoid the temptation to misuse your credit when other options are available. Overuse of debt can reduce your credit score and in turn increase the interest rates applied to all future debt. The result is that any future purchases that you finance will be more expensive. However, if you have a good history with the creditor, you may be in a position to receive better interest rates just by asking for it. If needed, you may even be able to ask for extensions to pay your bills. Your relationships with your creditors are valuable and long lasting, so nurture them as you would any personal relationship.

Principle in Action:

1. Identify two major goals that will have the most influence on the financial decisions you will make in your life.

2. Find one person that you will share your big picture objectives with so that they will keep you accountable.

Guiding Principle 6
You Must Have a Financial Plan for YOUR Life

No matter how much money you currently make, you can reach most of your financial goals if you have a plan and stick to it. For example, it is possible to retire comfortably with a steady income **starting** at just $10/hour. The less money you make, the more time and discipline you will need to reach your financial goals. Pay close attention to the assumptions outlined in this principle. The objective of this principle is to teach you some basic things to consider when planning for your future. After you have studied the scenario below, plug in your own numbers. Consider life events like marriage or the addition of children, which will have a dramatic impact on how your expenses will grow and how long it will take to retire. Ultimately, you will see how time can work in your favor, allowing you to meet your financial goals.

The most important part of any plan is being clear about your ultimate goal. If the goal is retirement, you have to calculate how much you have to save before you can retire. If you spend $2000 per month now, how much will you need to have saved to live for an additional 20 years without working? Without accounting for inflation, interest, or taxes, you would need approximately $480,000. You also want to consider what happens if you get sick or unable to take care of yourself, that $2000 a month can quickly rise to $4000 a month. Planning for retirement is a very personal and unique process for most people. Try to think from both extremes. How much do you need if everything goes as planned, and how much do you need if everything falls apart? Your retirement targets should be conservative, but somewhere between the extremes.

Let's see what would have to happen in order for someone making $10/hour today to retire comfortably. Note that all the numbers that follow in this plan only make sense with the assumptions that are stated. For example, the yearly adjustment for inflation is something you should monitor. If prices are going up, so should your salary. If your current position keeps you at the same salary, but the cost of living has increased 10% in the last 5 years, you should feel empowered to seek a raise or find another job that pays more. The assumptions are:

♦ **3% Inflation** adjustment is applied to the salary (annual raise) per year assuming no other promotions. Some employers who give inflation adjustments disguise this adjustment as an annual raise for performance. Although, your salary may double over 30 years, so will your expenses. The plan assumes that income and expenses grow at the same rate.

♦ **4% Savings rate** is typical for accounts that you can get at a credit union or bank savings account. You can save more by finding a higher interest bearing account, investing in IRAs, 401ks, or other tax-deferred options.

♦ **Shared expenses.** Many monthly costs can be reduced in half by having a roommate or by living with your parents. The following scenario assumes roommates or rental tenants.

♦ **Tax schedule for a single person.** The goal is to make purchases that help you reduce your tax burden, like mortgages instead of rent and investing in your own business.

Year 1 Assumptions:

To make this example work, a person making $10/hour should minimize expenses in any way possible. The early years will require you to have a roommate or live at your parent's home.

♦ **Rent -** Assume you live in a 2-bedroom $800/month apartment with one roommate; your half of the rent will be **$400/month**.
♦ **Groceries** – Your grocery bill will include the food you pack for lunch at work. **$250/month**
♦ **Utility Bills** – The assumption is that the only utilities you have are electric, gas, internet, water, phone. **$200/month**
♦ **Clothing/Entertainment** – This category includes clothing, dining-out, movies, and clubs. **$200/month**

♦ **Transportation** – For this plan, we will assume that you ride the bus to and from work. Avoid car loans if possible in the early years, even if you receive a car as a gift, the supplemental transportation costs may exceed $300/month for gas, insurance, parking, and maintenance. With a salary of $10/hour or less, try to find work close to where you live, so you can save more by walking or riding a bike to work. **$50/month**

♦ **Furniture** – For the sake of this exercise, the assumption is that will not buy any new furniture in your first year. Consider using old furniture from a family member or buy inexpensive furniture that you can upgrade when you have saved some money. Avoid any major furniture purchases or other similar credit expenses.

The key to succeed with less income is to stay ahead in the credit game. If you already have credit challenges, part of your budget will have to be dedicated to eliminating that debt, since debt costs you more than you will earn from any savings account. Let's look at the summary of your salary, spending and savings for the first year.

	Year 1	Year 3	Year 5
Salary	$20,800	-	-
Taxes	$2,755	-	-
Income after taxes	$18,045	-	-
Expenses	$13,200	-	-
Yearly Savings	$4,845	-	-
Interest from savings	$0	-	-
Savings Summary	$4,845	-	-
Principle paid	$0	-	-
Total Equity	$0	-	-
Potential House Value	$0	-	-

Year 3:
Assume all existing expenses remain, but because of inflation, they have increased by 3% each year. It is your responsibility to make sure your salary keeps up with the pace of inflation. By the end of Year 3, you should plan to put some of your savings into a down payment on your first house. Assuming a 15-year loan at 7% interest, you can buy a house under $100,000, with 10% down payment to keep your monthly mortgage around $800 a month. However if you continue to have a roommate (rental tenant), the net expense for mortgage remains $400/month. We will also add an assumption that you bought a house in an area of the city that has maintained steady growth and you will see an average appreciation of 3% each year on the value of the home.

	Year 1	Year 3	Year 5
Salary	$20,800	$22,066	-
Taxes	$2,755	$2,945	-
Income after taxes	$18,045	$19,121	-
Expenses	$13,200	$14,003	-
Yearly Savings	$4,845	$5,117	-
Interest from savings	$0	$400	-
Savings Summary	$4,845	$5,536	-
Principle paid	$0	$10,000	-
Total Equity	$0	$15,536	-
Potential House Value	$0	$100,000	-

Year 5:
Now that you have qualifying tax write-offs in a mortgage, state/local taxes, rental expenses, you will be able to afford a car loan or set aside a new savings account reserved for buying the car. One other good use of your savings is to pay extra principle on your mortgage to pay off the house

sooner. You will notice that the principle paid on the house will grow rapidly the longer you maintain the mortgage. By the nature of debt, you pay most interest when you first get the loan.

	Year 1	Year 3	Year 5
Salary	$20,800	$22,066	$23,410
Taxes	$2,755	$2,945	$2,256
Income after taxes	$18,045	$19,121	$21,154
Expenses	$13,200	$14,003	$14,856
Yearly Savings	$4,845	$5,117	$6,297
Interest from savings	$0	$400	$477
Savings Summary	$4,845	$5,536	$18,722
Principle paid	$0	$10,000	$17,292
Total Equity	$0	$15,536	$36,014
Potential House Value	$0	$100,000	$106,090

Years 10 through 40:

	Year 10:	Year 20:	Year 30:	Year 40
Salary	$27,139	$36,472	$49,016	$65,874
Taxes	$3,052	$5,783	$8,919	$13,133
Income after taxes	$24,087	$30,689	$40,097	$52,740
Expenses	$17,223	$23,146	$31,106	$41,804
Yearly Savings	$6,864	$7,543	$8,990	$10,935
Interest from savings	$1,992	$6,429	$ 13,414	$24,541
Savings Summary	$58,664	$174,708	$357,745	$649,008
Principle paid	$40,665	$100,000	$100,000	$100,000
Total Equity	$99,330	$274,708	$457,745	$749,008
Potential House Value	$122,987	$165,284	$222,128	$298,522

Assuming the 3% annual salary increase, you can see that your $10/hour job should now have an equivalent value of over $30/hour after 40 years of working. If you maintain the same salary over the course of several years, you are actually losing money, because even if your salary doesn't increase, your expenses will increase over time. The home you purchased at $100,000 could potentially be worth $300,000 depending on the location and maintenance of the house. With the outlined plan, after 40 years of work, you could retire with approximately one million dollars worth of assets, assuming you kept your expenses under control and made sure your salary grew. I understand you may think that some assumptions are unreasonable. In the above numbers, there is no mention of buying a car, having children or taking vacations. The only things discussed are paying bills, saving, and buying a house. The intent of showing you these numbers is just to give you a benchmark. If you want to live by yourself, drive a nice car, have children, and still retire with a similar cash reserve, you have to make more than $10/hour or find better ways to grow your money. There are many ways to reach your financial goals. Start to map out your own plan.

Principle in Action:

1. Identify how much more than $10/hour you have to make, in order to live the life you want.

2. Study any three careers to how salaries have grown over time. Research what the starting and average salaries were 10 and 20 years ago. Pay attention to salary growth when considering careers.

Tools

As you acquire better tools, the plans you develop will become more creative and require less effort to reach your goals.

Guiding Principle 7
Manage Pride, Emotion, and Your Money

This principle in no way advocates abandoning your convictions and moral standards. The idea is to make sure your emotions do not lead you to make decisions that are ultimately not in your best interest. Emotions tend to be unpredictable, while the key to financial success is consistency and growing money in a predictable fashion. All too often, emotion can also prevent you from taking full advantage of opportunities.

Use entry-level positions as stepping-stones. Do not be afraid to take an entry-level position that may not have the appeal or status you ultimately seek. It is difficult to find a job description that you would immediately think of as perfect. Often, finding a dream job is a function of how you evolve an existing job to take advantage of what you do best and what you enjoy. Entry-level jobs are necessary to get you in a position for the great things that you aspire to do. The key is to have a plan for moving up, and know that the entry-level position serves a specific purpose. Make friends and contacts in other parts of the organization. Volunteer to work on projects that extend beyond your area of expertise and accomplish a few "resume fillers." Unfortunately, most people do not think about their resume until they are ready to look for a new job. It is to your advantage to work on things that can eventually find their way onto your resume. Your previous job experience is like a story that you will have to sell one day to get a better job. Get the most out of each position.

Be open-minded. Before saying a job or profession is "beneath you," carefully consider the total compensation and freedom of that profession compared to what you see as an "ideal corporate job." Some good examples are jobs that require manual labor (painting, plumbing, flooring, or landscaping). Very often, a person in these fields can make an equivalent salary as someone in a corporate position, while working less hours. People in these fields have to be aggressive and always on the hunt for new business. The most compelling argument for independent business owners is, "the more they work, the more they make." In a salaried position, working 40 or 60 hours a week results in the same salary in the short term. The motivation to work longer hours is to give you a better chance of advancing in the company. The challenge is that as you climb the corporate ladder, there are few positions available for many qualified candidates. Therefore, ten people can put in 20 extra hours of work a week in order to have a chance at a higher salaried position, but they will all make the same money initially, and only one will get the promotion. If those same 10 people put 20 extra hours into their own independent businesses, their ability to increase both their short and long-term gains are higher. If you can tolerate the ups and downs of being independent, do not be afraid to consider the option.

Instead of being jealous, get motivated. Do not let jealousy keep you on the sidelines, criticizing those who are making more money than you are. Learn from what they are doing and provide them services they cannot provide for themselves. There are very few things in the world that only one person can do. Competition is at the heart of capitalism. If there is a person or company that has been successful, evaluate what it would take to compete or how you could expand their business with your own twist. Maybe you can reach customers they cannot. Perhaps, you can offer the same product or service at a lower price or deliver it in a different way.

Another way to leverage the wealth of the successful is to provide them goods and services. The truly wealthy are a very small percentage of the population, so there are few businesses that exist just to meet the needs of the wealthy. It is tough to start a business where you know that the market is small, but it can be very lucrative if you are able to deliver the right thing at the right time. In some cases, all it takes is that first client to get the ball rolling. Spend as much time building relationships as you do pushing your product or service. As the price of an item gets higher, trust becomes a bigger component of the buyer's thought process.

Don't be afraid to get help. Do not hide or avoid the things you do not do well, invest in someone who specializes in that area or get training to improve yourself. Many people allow the fear of failure or their perceived shortcomings to stop them from taking chances in business and investing. The key is to put together a team of people who compliment you (people who are strong where you are weak). It does not help much to surround yourself with people who are just like you. Beyond your friendships, be prepared to hire or buy time from "experts." Accountants, lawyers, financial planners, and marketing consultants can help you get the most out of your business or personal finances. Use them wisely because their services can be expensive. Choose these services based on references and their previous track record in successfully helping others. After you have found a good company, refer them to others. Helping them be successful and grow will inevitably help you too.

Try to minimize spontaneous and emotional purchases. There is a delicate balance between buyers and sellers. In the perfect case, the buyer makes a purchase when they need something and pays fair market value, and the seller prices the item at a price where he makes enough to cover all his costs and pocket a respectable profit. When that balance is disrupted, someone will end up on the losing end, usually the buyer. When a buyer makes an emotional connection to a product, they will likely pay more for it. It could be that they want to be the first to have an item, or they want to have the only one of that kind. Either way, that type of buyer will pay the most for a product. For some, that is not an issue. However, the average buyer will feel bad when they feel like they overpaid for something.

The other extreme is when the seller is desperate. Perhaps their inventory is too high or business has been very bad. The seller has to make drastic moves to get the product out of the door (big sales and discounts). As a buyer, you should pounce when the scales are in your favor. Buying things at a discount that you would have bought anyway is always a winning proposition.

Principle in Action:

1. Identify any areas where your emotions are restricting your ability to improve your financial standing. Focus on one area where you will attempt to tame your emotions.

2. Identify your weakest financial management skill and find ways to improve your skill level. Evaluate books and companies that focus on the area of concern.

Guiding Principle 8
Exercise Your Math Skills

When financial opportunities arise, the advantage goes to those who can make the best decisions quickly, often on very little information. To give yourself the best chance to compete, it is good to have some mathematical concepts and calculations that you commit to memory.

Estimate intelligently. One of the best things you can do is develop a method for estimating that works well for you. For example, rounding values to multiples of 10, 100, or 1000 is a great technique. You can even save yourself money, by always rounding up on your costs and rounding down on your revenue or income. Assume you have the option to buy a car that will cost $435 a month. As you try to consider if you can fit the item in your budget, think of it as a $500 a month expense. If you make $2250 a month after taxes, use $2000 as a reference value for your estimated income. Although, this technique is inappropriate for detailed budgeting, it will allow you to make quick decisions and protect yourself from getting in a cash flow crunch by overspending on spontaneous purchases.

Know your percentages. The easiest percentage value to remember is 10%. At the end of the day, calculating percentages boils down to multiplying and dividing. Percentages are easier to think of as division problems. For example:

50% of $100 = $100/2 = $50
25% of $100 = $100/4 = $25
20% of $100 = $100/5 = $20
10% of $100 = $100/10 = $10

As with most math concepts, there is usually more than one way to solve a problem. To determine what 10% of the original price is, just move the decimal place over by one place to the left.

10% of $300.00 = $30.00
10% of $11,000.00 = $1100.00
10% of $134,500.00 = $13,450.00

You can quickly find any multiple of 10% by multiplying the 10% value by the corresponding multiple.

20% = 2 x 10%
40% is 4 x 10%
30% of $300 = 3 x (10% of $300) = 3 x ($30) = $90
60% of $11000 = 6 x (10% of $11,000) = 6 x ($1100) = $6600

Once you are comfortable finding the 10% value, finding 5% is much simpler. 5% of something is just half of 10%

5% of $300 = (10% of $300)/2 = $30/2 = $15
5% of $11,000 = (10% of $11,000)/2 = $1100/2 = $550

By combining the concepts above, you can quickly do things like determine what a 15% penalty would be on a bill. Calculate 10% and 5% of the bill and add them together. You can also use "smart or safe estimation" when you have to determine a value that is not easy to calculate on the fly. If you have to quickly determine 27% of a value. Estimate with a lower percentage (25%) when considering how much you receive and use a larger percentage (30%) when you consider how much it you will have to spend. As you get more comfortable with the numbers, you quickly be able to realize that 27% is slightly less than halfway between 25% and 30%.

If you are able, always keep a calculator nearby. Many cell phones have calculators, so you may be in luck since you may always have one with you. The key is to never let the fear of "too many" numbers scare you away from making good decisions. Salespeople often prey on the natural tendency of people to look for simple answers. Too often, the simplest answers they present to you will most likely not be the best answer for you.

Compounding interest. A difficult concept for most people to grasp is compounding interest. It will affect both your savings and your borrowing, accelerating how quickly you gain wealth and increasing the rate at which your debt grows. Compounding interest means that the specified interest rate is applied to the original principal plus any previously accrued interest at regular intervals. The frequency of the compounding will increase the rate at which the principal grows. In the previous section, we discussed how to calculate percentages which is equivalent to evaluating simple interest. Simple interest yields a one-time return, while compound interest keeps on giving. The difference will be clear when you see the numbers.

The equation for compounding interest is:

$FV = PV \times (1 + I)^N$, where
FV is the calculated Future Value
PV is the original amount invested
N is the number of times the money is compounded

Assume the current value is $1000, Interest rate = 10%, Value is compounded annually.

Year 1: $FV = 100 \times (1 + .10)^1 = 100 \times 1.1 = \$110$
Year 2: $FV = 100 \times (1 + .10)^2 = 100 \times 1.21 = \$121$ *(+11)*
Year 3: $FV = 100 \times (1 + .10)^3 = 100 \times 1.33 = \$133$ *(+12)*
Year 4: $FV = 100 \times (1 + .10)^4 = 100 \times 1.46 = \$146$ *(+13)*
Year 5: $FV = 100 \times (1 + .10)^5 = 100 \times 1.61 = \$161$ *(+15)*

Notice that with each year, the Future Value is growing at a faster rate. The larger the Present Value, the more powerful compounding interest becomes to you. Even with a small original investment, earning anything from interest is better than keeping the money under your mattress. If you do not plan to spend the money soon, place it in an interest bearing account. Now watch what happens as the number of years goes up significantly.

Year 10: FV = 100 x (1 + .10)^{10} = 100 x 2.59 = \$259
Year 20: FV = 100 x (1 + .10)^{20} = 100 x 6.72 = \$672 *(+413)*
Year 30: FV = 100 x (1 + .10)^{30} = 100 x 17.44 = \$1,744 *(+1072)*
Year 40: FV = 100 x (1 + .10)^{40} = 100 x 45.25 = \$4,525 *(+2781)*
Year 50: FV = 100 x (1 + .10)^{50} = 100 x 117.39 = \$11,739 *(+7214)*

If you put \$100 into an account that grows at 10% a year for 50 years, it would be worth \$11,739 after 50 years. Imagine setting up investments for your grandchildren before you even have your first child. Time can really be your best friend when interest rates compound. Chasing wealth one generation at a time can be exhausting, if not impossible, so consider putting away some money for your grandchildren and great grandchildren.

Interest matters. Look at the following table showing how \$100 can grow over time. Notice how the column with 20% interest grows much faster than the 5% and 10% columns.

20% is a typical annual interest rate on most **credit cards**
10% is a good historical yearly return estimate for **stocks**
5% is the current average annual return on **savings** and **money market accounts**

	5%	10%	20%
Year 1	\$105.00	\$110.00	\$120.00
Year 3	\$115.76	\$133.10	\$172.80
Year 5	\$127.63	\$161.05	\$248.83
Year 10	\$162.89	\$259.37	\$619.17
Year 15	\$207.89	\$417.72	\$1,540.70
Year 25	\$338.64	\$1,083.47	\$9,539.62
Year 50	\$1,146.74	\$11,739.09	\$910,043.82

Although investing is important to growing wealth, controlling debt is even more important. Reconsider how much you are placing into retirement accounts if you are maintaining a credit card balance.

Tax assumptions. Tax calculations can get very complicated depending on how much you make and how many deductions you are able to claim. However, for decision-making purposes, it is good to be able estimate how much of your income goes to taxes. Previous tax returns are a good reference. For many people, assuming that one forth of your income will go to taxes is also a good estimate. Therefore, if someone tells you that a job will pay $50,000 a year, you can conservatively figure out that your take home pay will be around $37,500 or around $3000 a month.

Salary Math. Commit to memory how much you make per hour, week, month, and even your lifetime. Make decisions about your time and money in terms of how much the cost correlates with how much time you spend at your job to make that money. To figure out how much you make per day, week, month, and year, get comfortable with the conversions one stage at a time.

> Base Pay = $10/hour:
> Per day = $10/hour x **8 hours** = $80
> Per week = $80/day x **5 days** = $400
> Per month = $400/week x **4 weeks** = $1600
> Per year = $1600/month x **13 months** = $20800 (13 four-week months
>   make a 52-week year)

Considering the relationship between your time and money helps create the discipline needed to manage money effectively. You may think differently about spending a week's worth of income on something that you can only enjoy for one night. It is also good to have a reference for how much an hourly rate ultimately nets you per year. I am assuming a 40-hour workweek with 52 weeks in a year (Note: No taxes deducted).

> Monthly Income = Income/hour x 40hours/week x 4 weeks
> Yearly Income = Income/hour x 40 hours/week x 52 weeks
> $6/hour   >> $960 per month   >> $12,480   per year
> $10/hour >> $1600 per month >> $20,800   per year
> $30/hour >> $4800 per month >> $62,400   per year
> $50/hour >> $8000 per month >> $104,000 per year

Having these numbers in mind can help you place realistic expectations on what you can afford each month based on your potential salary. If you have a minimum wage job at $6/hour, it will limit your ability to live by yourself and afford luxury purchases.

Estimate how much money you will earn in your lifetime. Most people work somewhere between 40 and 50 years. Undoubtedly, you will receive promotions and raises along the way, but you can roughly estimate the money you will make in a lifetime by multiplying the yearly income by 50. The person making $6/hour will make approximately $600,000 in his lifetime. Someone making $10/hour will account for over $1,000,000 in a lifetime. The question will really be how much will you have left at the end of the race.

Principle in Action:

1. Set aside time to practice calculations involving interest and percentages. Use your investments and credit cards as the learning tool. Calculate how much you have spent or paid in interest in the past.

2. Make a personal goal to recognize percentage calculations without the use of a calculator or computer.

Guiding Principle 9
Credit is a Tool, Not a Solution

Credit is no different from any other financial tool, but for most people it is an obstacle that keeps them trapped in a painful cycle. Having credit means that some organization with free cash flow is willing to lend you money for a certain period, with a guarantee that you will pay them back with interest. If I loaned you $100 at 10% interest due back in 3 months, you would pay me back $110 after 3 months. The trick with credit is that the people who typically need the credit are those who will likely have the most difficult time paying it back. The more of a risk the borrower is, the more interest and restrictions the lender will place on the loan.

It sounds backwards, but you really should not seek most types of credit until you do not need it. Think about it. If you have used all your cash and have to borrow (use credit) to pay for something now, how likely is it that you will be able to pay back that money quickly. Credit card companies count on you taking a long time to pay back your debts. It may take you six months to pay off your debt, and each month, they make money from the interest you owe them. Be resourceful and creative. Instead of getting a credit card with a $2000 credit limit, save $200 a month for a year, and keep a special savings account where you maintain the $2400 balance. If you ever dip into that account, pay yourself back as you would a credit card company. Find ways to minimize your dependence on commercial credit.

How to establish credit – The measure most lenders use to determine your "credit-worthiness" is your payment history. Do you have a history of paying back your debts? Have you had any other credit cards? Have you had any utilities in your name? Whether you live at home or have roommates, start establishing your credit record by placing at least one bill in your name and making sure you are never late. Resist the temptation to get more credit than you need. Too many inquiries into your credit actually decreases your credit score. Even if you don't need the credit, it is in your best interest to have at least one card that you occasionally use and pay off immediately. If you have no credit history, you will have difficulty getting approval for apartments or home purchases when you need it.

How to repair credit – If you are ever in a position where you have ruined your credit, the first thing to do is understand how you got in that position. Paying back debt that you will only accumulate again is a frustrating cycle. Solutions like debt consolidation only work if you decrease or stop spending. Try to pinpoint the habits or situations that caused you to spend money that was not budgeted and attack that first.

Once you have tamed the spending beast within you, try to pay off the lowest balance you have. If your balances are similar across many lenders, compare the interest rates and pay off the debt with the highest interest rate first. Unless you have no other choice, never pay just the minimum payment. Avoid managing your finances by the minimum and maximum amounts given to you by a lender. Always pay more than the minimum and never use the maximum credit they give you. When you pay off one card, lock the card away in a safe, but keep the account open. Having an unused balance can boost your credit score, giving you better interest rates for something like a house.

Use credit like a business would – Most successful businesses have to leverage credit to grow their businesses. Companies borrow money at a low interest rate to finance operations that grow money at a faster rate. An example could be a car company who keeps $200 million in cash and wants to build a new plant that costs $100 million. They might borrow $100 million to build the new plant at an interest rate of 10% a year. If products from that plant return a profit of at least $20 million each year, then the company will be able to pay back the principle and interest on the loan within 7 years. The company would simultaneously invest some of the $200 million in short-term investments that also generate additional revenue. The fact that the company has $200 million in assets will also motivate lenders to give the company better interest rates.

For most of us, we use credit to buy something that we want now, not considering how the extra money we are paying in interest should be offset

Guiding Principle 9

by a greater return. If you own a small business, you may put a new printer on a credit card if that extra printing capacity allows you to double your profits. Try to ask yourself this question each time you pull out a credit card, "how will financing this purchase help me make more money?"

Credit cards have made it easy to delay paying the full price for items you want to get now. However, in using credit, you typically pay more for the item than it is worth. One reason to offer a consumer instant credit approval on purchases is because there is a small window to charge top dollar for an item. Getting you to buy early is a goal of any business. Many people punish themselves twice when making purchases at their highest price, using a high interest credit card. Credit serves a fundamental purpose in any society; the key is to use credit to help you get ahead.

Principle in Action:

1. Request your current credit report. Verify any outstanding debts on your report. Calculate your total debt.

2. Distinguish the debt that allows you to make more money from the debt that does not. Work harder to eliminate the debt that is not allowing you to make more money while you defer payments.

3. Research additional ways to leverage credit to increase your earning power. Small business loans and college tuition loans are common examples.

49

Investing

Investing is a lifestyle that teaches you to value everything you have. Those assets that have the greatest potential for growth deserve your focused attention and energy.

Guiding Principle 10
Develop the Mindset of an Investor

The skills you need to make good financial decisions will benefit you in all areas. Exercising discipline and patience with each decision gives you the best chance to control your future. Establish your own rules for what makes a good investment (or decision). Know when, how, and why to get out of an investment. Finally, learn how to create something that others will want. Here are a few things to consider, as you become an investor:

An investment is anything that you acquire that has the potential of growing in value. The question you have to continually ask is, "what am I getting compared to what I am giving up?" The relationships that work in your life have a clear give and take. If you feel like you do all the giving and never receive anything, you might question why you invest your resources into an investment that yields no return. If you vote for a political candidate, but they never take actions that benefit you as a constituent, you will not vote for that person again. As you consider educational expenses, choose options that increase your marketability and earning potential, or give you a distinct non-financial reward that has value to you. If having the degree does not have a return that you can use, the investment of your time, energy, and money may sting just a bit more.

If the "investment" does not have a clear expected return, it is not an investment. The return might not always be financial, but the investment has to give you something back that you feel is worthwhile. Smart investors are very clear on what the expected return will be before ever investing the first dollar. Investing should never be about guessing. A loan is an investment. If you give someone a loan, you are making an investment with the expectation that the borrower can pay you back the principle plus whatever interest you apply. If you are serious about receiving payback, enter into loans with an understanding of how risky the transaction could really be and exactly how much you expect back over time.

One tricky thing to watch out for is so-called investments where you get your return upfront. It is not an investment if you get all the value from the item when you purchase the item. Most people are willing to spend more for items that they consider investments. Many salespeople will present their items as "investments" for this reason. Ask yourself, "Will this item grow in value?" If not, it is not an investment.

Maintain a watchful eye on risk. Since the consequences of financial choices can have a lifelong impact (especially when things go wrong), it is critical that you have solid rules for making investments. The goal is to make your financial future as predictable as possible. There are a few basic concepts to consider and customize to your situation.

1. There is a direct correlation between Risk and Reward. The higher the potential reward, the more risk will be involved. Risk means there is a chance that you will suffer a loss. An investment in a savings account in an FDIC insured bank has essentially no risk, protecting up to the first $100,000. The return you will get from a savings account will in turn be relatively low. An investment in a new company that has a great idea, but no revenue, would fall on the other end of the risk spectrum. You could easily lose your whole investment if the company fails or greatly multiply your initial investment if all goes as planned. The following are a few simple questions that will help you evaluate the risk associated with an investment. Add as many additional questions as you need to be comfortable.

   a. How much will this "investment" cost me in total? (Not just how much up front, but also consider any fees or tax implications).

   b. How long will it take me to receive my payback?

   c. What is the history of the investment? Is it an asset with a history of growth? Alternatively, does the value of the investment show any trends? Up or down?

d. Do I have a way out if the investment outlook begins to turn negative?

e. What additional liabilities am I taking on? What happens to me if the company does something unethical or illegal?

f. Where do I fall in the payback line? (Are there other more "important" investors who are paid first, potentially delaying or diluting how much I make?)

Your comfort level with questions like this should dictate how much you invest or loan. If you are not even willing to ask the questions, you are likely letting emotion direct you instead of financial logic. Taking on some risk is not bad, but you should never let your risk be open-ended (know the limits of how much you are willing to lose).

2. You can manage your risks. Financial advisors often talk about diversifying your portfolio. Even if you do not have any investments, you can still apply the same concepts to your daily financial decisions. Every dollar you spend is an investment for which you expect to get something in return. Diversification means you mix where you place your money. The mix should be a function of your long and short-term goals and your personal threshold for risk. The biggest challenge for most new investors is that all their goals tend to be short-term. They expect to see immediate success or they give up. As a beginner, lean more toward lower risk investments that allow you to build confidence as an investor. Your primary goal is to achieve consistent financial results. No matter how much money you have, you can start practicing the habits of a good investor.

3. Once the investment has reached your desired value, cash out or reinvest into something else that has more growth potential. You become a more powerful investor when you cultivate the art of selling at the right time. The key is to define your sell price ahead of time. You may not always sell at the very highest point, but if you meet your objectives, you never lose. It is tempting to think that a house will be worth more next year or that a stock will keep going up, but try to

maintain your discipline. Since investments can lose value, you must also have a minimum threshold for when you will sell. It is much cheaper to cut your loses and try again later.

Be able to create a profitable investment. The ultimate evidence that you have learned how to make good investments is when you create a product, service, or business that others consider as a good investment. It could be a company, a non-profit charitable organization, or even a fund where others simply give you their money to invest for them (mutual funds). Even if you don't need additional investors, run your business as if you did. Develop a clear plan for how the company will grow. Think specifically about what short and long-term returns an investor could expect to see.

When you are committed to a particular cause or ideal, you should consider applying what you have learned and practiced about investing to a non-profit organization. Too often, well-intentioned people will start a non-profit business, without actually knowing anything about how to run a business or how to raise money. Supporting a non-profit can go far beyond donations and community service projects. The leaders of the organization may be too proud to ask for help directly, but if you see problems that you have the skills to solve, volunteer your services. Keeping the organization functional is just as important as the service itself.

As you develop a record of accomplishments that highlight your ability to make good investment decisions, others will want to trust you with their assets. If you have been successful investing stocks with your personal assets, you could take the test to become a licensed broker. Being licensed can quickly multiply the number of career options you will have. You might even consider starting your own firm and providing financial services for other people. Continue to build upon what you have learned and embrace new challenges.

Principle in Action:

1. Buy or check out a book from the library specifically about how to invest in Stocks, Bonds, or Options.

2. Identify two companies that you will watch as a potential investor. Read their quarterly and annual reports. Identify the things you do not understand and make homework assignments for you to research that information.

3. Evaluate all your possessions and determine how many qualify as investments. Find out the current value of each investment and try to determine if the value can still grow.

4. Dedicate an hour a week to find new potential investments and rank each one according to their potential value and risk.

Guiding Principle 11
Invest in Yourself

In order to maximize your earning potential, you are going to have to make many investments where the return will not be financial. The primary example is the money you spend to educate yourself. The idea of spending over $10,000 each year for a college degree can be very intimidating. However, your future salary will likely be higher than what it would have been without a college degree.

A college degree does not indicate how smart or capable you are, but it often serves as ticket to many of the places you want to go. Most managerial jobs will have some minimal education requirement. In many careers, increasing levels of education correlate to higher earning potential. You can choose from four-year colleges, junior colleges, technical schools, and several other continuing education options. The key is to know your end goal before you start chasing random degrees. You also need to exhaust all options for paying for an education. The following are some of the most common methods:

♦ **Scholarships** – A scholarship is FREE money. You qualify for a scholarship based on academic performance. Grades, test scores, and essays will often determine how much scholarship money you will get. Consider scholarship money as tax-free income that will help you make more money. Thinking of it as income can force you to see formal education as a job. As with any job, if you do not perform, you will lose your scholarship, your income, your revenue. There is a little more at stake here than "free money." A scholarship frees the student up to just focus on academics. The best time to get this money is in the Junior and Senior year of high school.

Students should aggressively focus on becoming eligible for as many scholarships as possible. Something as simple as a $200 SAT/ACT review course or even a $30 review book could make the difference in being eligible for over $100,000 in scholarships. If you score above certain values on the SAT and maintain at least a 3.0 G.P.A, you can get a full scholarship to many colleges.

Consider adding scholarship preparation money in your budget. Becoming eligible for the best scholarships takes time and money. Introduce eighth and ninth graders to SAT/ACT preparation courses. Encourage them to take classes in high school that supplement test preparation, like Latin and Algebra. Research the available scholarships that you can use for motivation long before you need them.

Some students qualify for scholarships with their other talents and activities. These include scholarships in athletics, visual/performing arts, and community service. Even if you have no interest in careers specifically related to your talents, use that talent to finance your education. As with an academic scholarship, being a collegiate athlete or performer will be a job. Not only will you have to perform at the top of your game, but you will also need to maintain high academic standards. Having the discipline to manage both will make you an excellent candidate for the career of your choice.

◆ **Grants** – Grants are slightly different from scholarships in that grants are based upon financial need and academic performance. Grants can come from national, state, and specific school-related organizations. When you apply to different schools, also investigate the criteria for qualifying for grants. With the help of grants and scholarships, even Ivy League schools (Harvard, Yale, Princeton, etc) are not out of reach for any aspiring college student. Grants often cover specific areas of study or research, so a little investigation can help you find the perfect scenario to get your education paid for. In general, grants are underused. Every year, thousands of grants go unclaimed, simply because no qualified candidates are available. Income does not have to be an obstacle to higher education. Most of the money given by way of grants comes from federal Pell Grants (Pell Grants are usually reserved for undergraduate students only).

♦ **Loans** – If you are unable to get enough money in scholarships and grants to finance your education, you may have to get a loan. Federal Student loans have some of the most favorable terms of any type of loan. Some benefits include lower interest rates and deferred payments. The benefit of deferment is that you do not have to start paying back the loan until after you finish your education, even if you go to graduate school. The downside of deferment is that in most cases, the unpaid interest on the loan continues to grow while you are in school. As with any debt, if you wait too long to pay it back, the size of the debt grows rapidly. Subsidized Stafford loans are one example of a loan that has no accrued interest or prepayment penalties. Loan options like mortgaging your home, bank loans, or using credit cards are less desirable. They typically cost you significantly more in the end. If you are resourceful and committed, do not be afraid to seek financing from family members, mentors, or even peers. Family members may be willing to offer you low or no interest loans to help you get through the education process.

Loans from the government for education tend to be more accommodating than anything you could get directly from a bank. Besides deferment, they may also offer lower interest rates (not a function of your credit score) and longer terms for repayment. Some examples of federal loans are the Perkins Loan, Subsidized and Unsubsidized Stafford Loan, and the PLUS loan (Federal Parent Loan for Undergraduate Students). The Perkins loan is only available to students whose household income is below a predetermined amount. Subsidized Stafford loans are distributed based on the student's financial need, but the government pays the interest on the loan while the student is in school. Upon graduation, you will assume all repayment responsibilities. An Unsubsidized Loan is not need-based, so everyone is eligible no matter how much the family income is. The catch with unsubsidized loans is that you will be responsible for paying the interest on the loan while you are in school. If you do not pay it in a timely manner, the interest accrues and is added to the original loan amount. So when you do begin repayment, you start with a larger balance. The PLUS loan is a low interest loan available to parents of an undergraduate student.

♦ **Working Student** – When scholarships, grants, and loans are not sufficient to pay for school, many students work while in school. This route takes extreme dedication and discipline. Often, it results in the student having to enroll as a part-time student, either because the job demands too much of their time, or they can only afford a few hours of tuition each semester. Although finding a way to make this option work says a lot about you and your work ethic, continue to look for ways to supplement your income to lessen the stress on you. If you do not qualify for Student Aid one year, try again the next. Getting a $2000 loan after your first year of school at a 5% interest rate (deferred until after graduation), could save you 200 hours of working a job at $10/hour.

Work Study programs are jobs included in a financial aid package to assist in paying tuition costs. Work Study jobs are often great because they allow you to work for the university. Some university jobs have hidden benefits that will not show up in the paycheck. For example, work-study in a library or a computer lab can give you time and exposure to work with resources that most students never know about.

Co-op programs are another great way for students to finance their education and gain practical experience while pursuing a degree. In most Co-op programs, the student alternates between work and school each semester or quarter. One semester you are in class full time, and the next semester you will work full time. One of the main benefits of co-ops is that you do not have to try to juggle school and work at the same time. Typically, students will be required to get jobs that relate to their degree, allowing them to gain real-world experience before they even graduate. A possible drawback is that it may take longer than the traditional four years to finish, but the actual time in class and the cost of your education would be the same. In addition, by the time a co-op student graduates, they will have more work experience than their fellow graduates, making them more attractive in the job market.

♦ **Tuition Reimbursement programs at a job** – One of the best benefits to look for when taking a job is the existence of a tuition reimbursement program. In most programs, you will have to pay the initial tuition, and if you pass with an acceptable grade, the company will reimburse the money you spent.

If you have to choose between a job that pays $10/hour with Tuition reimbursement and a job that pays $12/hour without the same benefit. I argue you take the job that pays less. In a year, the first job will pay you $20,800 before taxes ($15,600 after taxes – assuming 25% tax). The second job will pay $24,960 before taxes ($18,720 after taxes). The difference would be $3120 in take home pay. Tuition reimbursement packages range in value, but they typically are in step with the IRS limit for how much a company can give you and still get a tax write-off. Assume that the tuition limit was $5200. By taking the first job and taking advantage of the tuition reimbursement program, you have made a net gain of over $2000. In addition, companies can offer you more than the tax-free amount, but you would have to pay the tax on that expense. Either way, any kind of tuition reimbursement program is a benefit you have to utilize.

One of the least publicized yet wonderful ways to finance an education is to work in a school system. Many schools not only offer discounts and free tuition to the employee, but also to the children of their employees. There may be limitations on which schools you can attend, but a free education is tough to turn down.

That is just the beginning. By pursuing further education, you have increased your earning potential. Upon completing your degree, you will be eligible for additional jobs, many of which will give you greater responsibilities and an increased salary.

Principle in Action:

1. Identify two ways you can increase your earning potential by educating yourself.

2. Find three grants or scholarships that you are eligible for and apply. Many will require some type of essay. Set aside a few hours a week to apply for scholarships.

Guiding Principle 12
Use Money to Make More Money

The secret is that you do not have to have millions before you can apply this principle. Two of the most profitable and most enduring institutions in the world are banking and insurance. To state it simply, they take the large sums of money they have accumulated to make more money. Both use compounding interest to drive their profits. Compounding interest allows money to grow at a faster rate the longer you hold it. It is the reason that a 30-year loan on a $100,000 house at 7% will really cost you $240,000 over the 30 years, allowing the bank to make $140,000 in profit.

With insurance, it is a little harder to see the correlation. The only reason they can offer you coverage is that they have money to start with. Think about how much you pay each month in insurance premiums and compare that with how much you really get out of it. A car insurance company may charge you $100/month for the ability to have them pay off any damage you may have or cause while driving. If you never have an accident, over 30 years, the insurance company has made $36,000. If you do have an accident and they have to incur a payout, your premium will go up significantly, depending on how much they had to spend. When you have speeding tickets, you are actually giving them free money, because they can increase your premium because you are now a greater risk. The insurance company understands the likelihood of having to pay on a claim and they will charge you so that over the long haul, they will always make more than they spend. As you accumulate wealth, you will have more opportunities to grow your money and reduce your expenses. There are several ways that you can leverage the money you have to your benefit:

♦ **Buy things that grow in value over time**. Simplify the concept of investing. If all the evidence tells you that something will be worth more in a year or 10 years than it is worth today, you should consider buying it. That is the basic concept of buying and selling real estate and stocks. Those with the money to buy things when they are undervalued stand to make the most money, so it is always smart to keep some money "liquid" (that just means money that you can access without penalties or fees whenever you are ready). History is often the best indicator of what an investment will do, so be prepared to dig around before giving up your money. If there is no history to base your decision on, you can still invest, but do so with less money than you would something that has a history of excellent performance.

♦ **Buy higher volumes to reduce your unit costs**. If you are a business or an individual who buys items for use or sale, buy in bulk if you can afford to. Most of the time, you will get some kind of volume discount. At the very least, you should ask for one. In many cases, it costs more to keep items on the shelf than to sell them for a slightly lower price. Speak in ways that makes sense to the person you are buying from.

♦ **Use your available money to make larger down payments or to reduce debt**. Down payments are more than just minimum requirements when making a purchase. They really work in your favor when used correctly. Any money you can put down will save you from paying extra interest. Unless that money is making more money in another account with a higher interest rate than what you are paying on the loan, add it to your down payment. Do not pay more in interest than you have to. If you are already paying high interest on a loan or credit cards, use any extra money you have to pay on the principle so that you can reduce how much money you give away in interest. Balancing debt and savings is tough, but if you have $500 in a savings account returning 3%, but you have $500 on a credit card that charges 20%, take the money out of savings and pay off the debt.

♦ **Offer cash to get immediate discounts on large purchases**. If you have had the discipline or the fortune to accumulate large sums of money, recognize that cash by itself is a bargaining chip. When purchasing a car or a home, you can often negotiate a lower price if you have the ability to pay in cash. Most vendors have to pay fees or interest when they finance something for you. The company will pass on any additional costs they incur to you in the price. In addition, a vendor would prefer to get as much of his money up front as possible.

◆ **Reduce insurance premiums as you pay off property/cars.** Learn how to be more critical of what you are paying for in your insurance premiums. Raising your deductible can significantly reduce how much your monthly premium will cost you. If you have a $500 deductible, but have $500 in the bank that you can leave untouched, raise your deductible to $1000. If you have to file a claim, you already have the extra money saved. If you avoid any problems, you could save $10 to $20 per month in insurance. Within a couple of years, you have saved enough money to free up the $500 you saved. Having extra cash puts you in a position where you do not have to rely on others as much in the event that something bad happens, so do not pay for insurance you don't need.

◆ **Invest in building your network.** As you make money consider making purchases that open you to new opportunities or introduce you to people who have shown an ability to make money. Join a social club or country club and surround yourself with other people that have achieved similar levels of success. Membership at such clubs can be very expensive, but you might meet the person who leads you into a million dollar contract. Even if you do not get any direct business, you can learn many things just by playing golf with a retired CEO or a successful entrepreneur. You may not be able to buy success, but you can buy a ticket to the place where the successful play.

◆ **Help meet the needs of the less fortunate.** Beyond the obvious social, emotional, and tax benefits for being charitable, there are economic reasons to share your wealth. A healthy economy recycles money. If too many people sit on their earnings and stop spending or giving, the entire economy slows down. Enable others to be successful, and you will continue to be successful. Do more than just send a contribution. Attend or volunteer at events hosted by charities and meet the other attendees. Charity dinners, silent auctions, banquets, and other volunteering events provide excellent opportunities to meet and interact with all kinds of people.

♦ **Become a lender, not a borrower.** When you are able to accumulate money, consider finding a way to make more by lending to those capable of paying you back. There is a difference between giving to a charity and being a lender. Do not lend with just the hope of repayment. Provide the borrower with terms that protect you, such as significant down payments, escalating late fees, and swift loss of collateral. Some terms may sound harsh, but if the borrower is dedicated to being a good customer, you will not scare them off. You want borrowers who have something to lose, people who value their reputation and have worked to achieve a good credit history. You can compete with bigger banks and lenders, so compete for the good customers. If you want to walk the line of being a lender to riskier borrowers, protect yourself with the terms you set.

Principle in Action:

1. Evaluate what you are doing with any money you have saved. Identify two ways you can invest that money or use it to reduce your debt.

2. Research a career that demonstrates this principle (Banking, Insurance, and Bail Bondsman). Consider job opportunities, even if they are entry level, and learn how they make money grow.

Guiding Principle 13
Know Your Financial Investment Options

Deciding what to do with your money for short and long term periods is really a function of your personality, timing, and objectives. No matter how much or how little money you have, you should always know your options for making your money work for you. Each investment option has varying levels of restrictions and many investments have penalties associated with any early withdrawal of funds. Some penalties are good because they force you to save more money for later in life.

When looking at your options, one of the first things that will stand out is the interest rate (or rate of return) associated with the investment. You will often see the interest rate expressed as APR (Annual Percentage Rate) or APY (Annual Percentage Yield). APR is what you will likely see most often. It is the interest rate that the financial institution quotes that does not take into account the impact of compounding interest. APY is the total amount of interest including compounding interest. If the interest is compounding once a year, the values will be the same, but if the interest is compounded monthly (credit cards) or quarterly, the difference between APR and APY will be larger. When investing, you want to seek investments that have larger APY value.

After the interest rate, the next most significant factor in how much you make is how much you invest. A 5% rate of return may not appear that attractive when you only have $1000 to invest. The net return will be $50. However, if you invest $20,000 with the same 5% rate, you will make $1000. Too many people with smaller initial investments get discouraged because it is difficult to see the value of investing soon enough. When you don't have much to invest in the beginning, time has to be your primary weapon. With a 5% interest rate, it will take 15 years to turn that $1000 into $2000. However, if you put in an extra $100 a year on top of your original investment, after 15 years, you will have over $4000. The temptation when you do not have much to invest is to take bigger risks, but there are few shortcuts for making money. Whether you have $100 or $100,000, be patient and consistent with your investments. Here are some of the options to consider.

1. **Bank Accounts** - At the very least, open a savings and checking account. Most banks and financial institutions offer some type of free savings or checking accounts. If you have a tendency to overspend, place some of your money in a savings account. They often have restrictions on how many times you can access your account, which can actually help you save more money.

   One of the main benefits of maintaining a checking account is free check cashing and check writing. Without an account, you could easily lose hundreds of dollars over the course of a year just cashing checks and buying money orders. Opening multiple accounts also allows you to keep more of your money out of reach. Discipline yourself to withdraw a set amount of cash each month to make it easier to track your spending.

   Be careful with debit cards. In many ways, the convenience of a debit card can be the fastest way to drain your account. When people had to write checks for everything, those who balanced their checkbooks saw the daily impact of their spending. With a debit card, you can easily empty your checking account and not realize the damage until the end of the month. To force yourself into disciplined habits with debit cards, try to withdraw the cash you need each week and minimize the use of the debit card. Another option is to maintain a separate savings account that allows you to easily transfer money between the checking and savings account. Use a free online banking account to transfer money out of your checking account to restrict your ability to overspend. Very few of us have the self-control to consistently make the right financial decisions. Sometimes, you simply have to make it more difficult to get to your money to help you save the most money.

2. **Certificate of Deposit (CD)** – A CD is a deposit that you make to a bank or financial institution for a set time for a predetermined rate of return.

The typical periods are from 3 months to 5 years. The longer the term of the CD, the higher the interest rate the bank will give you. CDs will offer you a better rate of return than a savings account, but historically not as much as the stock market (CDs are less risky than stocks).

3. **Treasuries** – These savings options come directly from the government. They are essentially tools that the U.S. Government uses to finance debt, but they can also help you effectively save money.

   a. Treasury bills (T-bills) have terms up to a year and are sold at a discount from their face value, making them possibly the least risky investment option. For instance, you might pay $480 for a $500 bill. When the T-bill matures, you will receive a payment of $500. The value of the interest is what dictates the difference between the purchase price and face value.
   b. Treasury notes (T-Notes) can be issued for two, three, five, and 10-year terms and earn a fixed interest rate every six months until maturity. The fact that the notes compound twice a year makes this investment more valuable than a CD with the same interest rate or even one with a slightly lower interest rate.
   c. Treasury bonds are issued for 10 years or more. They compound every 6 months and can provide a fixed interest rate for up to 30 years. Treasury will auction 30-year bonds twice a year, in February and August. Treasury bonds are great savings tools for people who want to make sure that their children have a good head start when they become adults.

4. **Stocks** – In the simplest terms, to buy a stock in a company is to buy part of that company. The more shares you buy, the more of the company you own. Corporations can be either public or private. Shares of public companies can be acquired and traded through brokerage firms, mutual funds, IRAs, or 401k plans. Private companies do not trade or sell their shares on the open market. Typically, publicly traded corporations issue some of their stock for purchase by the general public and investment funds. The remaining shares of stock are distributed among employees. Stock distributions serve as incentives to drive

employees to work harder. If you join a company and receive stock options, the more the company grows, the value of your stock options will grow. Try to remember that the primary reason for having stock is to finance operations. Companies issue stock in the place of compensation and in exchange for debt. Although issuing some new stock is normal, be wary of investing in companies that constantly issue new stock.

Buying and selling stocks can be tricky, but it is not something that you have to be afraid to try. If you are a disciplined investor, you will have a better chance of success than if you enter this arena as a stock trader. An investor would be someone who buys a stock with long-term returns in mind. Suppose you buy a stock that you expect to increase by 10% each year for the next 3 years, but it gains 10% in 6 months. An investor will continue to hold on to the stock because they have purchased the stock with a 3-year window in mind, or the equivalent 33% return. Successful investors know their goals and live by those goals rather than the emotions associated with what they see in the day-to-day market swings. On the other hand, a trader is more likely to sell after 6 months, incur the higher tax rate, and cash out his profits right away instead of waiting to see what may happen down the road. A trader tries to keep as much of his cash available as possible to capitalize on every new opportunity that presents itself. Active trading involves significantly more risk, since stocks can experience significant short-term peaks and valleys. If you are a beginner, try to look for stocks that have great long-term potential (more than 3 years of potential growth).

The art of learning if and when to buy a stock is a very involved subject that can have completely different answers depending on who you talk to. My abbreviated summary is simple; unless you have some kind of special knowledge about what the future of a company holds, rely on the past to give you a sense of where the company is going. Has the company made money or is it all about 'potential'? Does it keep costs under control? Do they have many competitors? Do they dilute their shares with debt? Do they have a habit of over-promising and not delivering? Who else is investing in them? Do the Insiders (employees) buy or sell the stock with regularity? Questions like this can help you see which direction a company is going.

The next tough question is at what price do I buy? Some stocks are cyclical, meaning they have moderately consistent peaks and valleys. If you can buy while they are down and have the discipline to wait for the next up turn, you will make money. Some stocks move aggressively on rumors, so some traders/investors start buying on the first hint of "something new" and sell after the company delivers. Many investors use the price to earnings (P/E) ratio as a guide. This simply refers to the relationship between the price of the stock and the earnings per share they deliver. In some cases, a stock with a P/E ratio significantly lower than its peers could be a bargain.

There are very few easy answers when it comes to investing in stocks, but one clear answer is you cannot make any money if you are on the sidelines. As you learn more about money, I recommend finding 3 to 5 companies that you are interested in and study them for a year. Don't put any money into this "research project" right away. Subscribe to any free site that sends you email updates any time this company has a press release or earnings announcements. Learn how to read the press releases for clues about the company's future direction. Scan the earnings for how much cash they have in the bank and how well they are improving margins. Then watch how these announcements affect the rise or fall of the stock price. You may be surprised to see that after many announcements, the price will drop even when the news is good. Find out why. Sometimes, it is because the news was anticipated for so long, the stock already climbed. There could be many reasons.

Your ability to answer "why" will help you become a successful investor. Choose companies from different industries, with different levels of development (a new company vs. a firm over 50 years old). Treat this research as you would a class and dedicate at least an hour a week just to study. It may sound like unnecessary work, but after years of working hard, you will appreciate having options for making money, that do not require as much of your time and energy.

5. **Mutual Funds** – A mutual fund is a collection of stocks that are managed by a person or financial institution. Examples are growth fund or an income fund. Each fund will consist of stocks with some common attributes. A growth fund includes stocks expected to grow at a faster rate than the norm, but also have a slightly higher risk. An income fund may consist of stocks that many not grow very fast, but have shown a history of stable predictable growth, making the purchase less risky. By definition, a mutual fund is somewhat diversified already, but you can always buy multiple funds with different objectives and further diversify your investments.

    At least twice a year, you should check the performance of your mutual funds against other funds to see if it is competing well with funds managed by other firms. You have every right to place your money in the best performing funds. Ideally, your fund should outperform the general market. Standard market measuring sticks include the S&P 500 (collection of 500 of the top companies), the NASDAQ 100 (collection of 100 of the top technical companies in the world), and the Dow (collection of 30 specific companies that serve as a representation of all major industries). With the introduction of Index Funds, it is easier for every investor to buy a collection of stocks that share some common characteristic. Index funds are generally cheaper than mutual funds because you can purchase them as you would any single stock. There is far less management required by the broker because the fund mimics existing indices, like the S&P 500, NASDAQ 100, or Russell 2000.

6. **401k Savings Plan** – 401k plans are a way to save money for retirement, which allow you to reduce your short-term tax liability. The amount of money that the employee contributes to the plan is deducted from the taxable income reported to the IRS. For example if you make $50,000 a year and contribute $10,000 to the 401k plan, your taxable income is $40,000 instead of $50,000. Contributions to 401k plans have an annual cap, which up until 2005 has been $12,000 per year. This amount is subject to change per changes in the tax code. After contributing to the 401k fund, the employee will have choices for where to invest the money within the fund. Typically, people will invest into mutual funds, bond

funds, or employee stock option plans. You should choose a different type of fund depending on where you are in your career. In the early years, your choices would be more aggressive than when you are closer to retirement. Aggressive (growth) funds have larger swings between good years and bad years, so you do not want retirement to occur during a down year.

The plans will allow your money to grow tax-free until the employee is 59 ½. If you withdraw the money early, an additional 10% penalty will be applied on top of the taxes that will be due upon withdrawing the profits from the 401k. As with any other investment that you have held for over a year, 401k plans will be eligible for the reduced capital gains tax of 15% (20% after 2013) instead of the normal income tax rate, which can rise to over 40%.

One of the most attractive things about 401k plans is that most large companies will match part of what the employee contributes. For example, imagine your company says they will match 100% of the first 3% of the employee's contribution to a 401k plan. If you make $50,000 a year, the company doubles your 401k investment up to $1500 a year. You can still contribute up to $12,000 a year on your own, but the company will add an additional $1500 to your contribution for a maximum of $13,500 a year. If you choose good funds, that contribution can grow steadily until you retire. Assume you contribute to the 401k for 30 years, with an average yearly return of 8%; the maximum contribution will turn into over $1.5 million dollars for retirement. Even if you pay the 20% capital gains tax when you retire, you will still have over $1.2 million for retirement.

7. **Individual Retirement Account (IRA)** – An IRA is a personal retirement account that the investor can control. IRAs are similar to 401k plans in that they provide a tax deferred way to invest into stocks and bonds. Traditional IRAs differ from Roth IRAs because the investor pays taxes at different points in the investment cycle. With a traditional IRA, the investor is able to deduct contributions to the IRA from their taxable income each year. When they are ready to cash out of the investment

after age 59 ½, they will pay the capital gains tax on the profits over the life of the investment. A Roth IRA does not offer the short-term tax break because the investor invests money after taxes are paid. However, when the profits are cashed out at retirement, no taxes will be due. In short, the investment grows tax free, making the Roth IRA a very attractive option. The rules for when and how much you can contribute to an IRA account can differ depending on each year's IRS policy. One major difference between IRAs and 401ks is the difference in the amount that you can contribute each year. Therefore, even though the IRA might grow tax free, you will not be able to invest as much in an IRA as you would a 401k. For 2006, the IRA limit for people under age 50 is $4,000 and over age 50 is $5000. While the limit for a 401k is $15,000 under age, 50 and $20,000 over age 50.

Deciding which option is right for you has to be a function of what your goals are. Is the money being saved for retirement? Is it money for your children? Are you just trying to diversify where you invest your money? Since these investments are long term, you want to make the deposits as soon as you are able to, but you also want to get as much FREE advice as you can. Financial institutions compete for a chance to manage your money, so play your part and make them show you why they deserve that right. Being a knowledgeable investor can only help you get the best solutions at the end of the day. Ask questions. There are no bad questions when it comes to your money.

Principle in Action:

1. Take advantage of at least two investment options, even if you just open the accounts with the minimum amount allowed.

2. Spend at least an hour per week thinking, planning, or making choices about investing.

Originality

Have the courage to review how you think about making and spending money, then develop rules and standards you can live by.

Guiding Principle 14
Create Your Own Financial Progress Card

If you spend your life evaluating how successful you are by looking at other people, you can easily become frustrated and lose motivation. The key to maintaining your peace of mind in this journey is focusing any judgment or definitions of success inward. Set your own financial goals that you will use to evaluate your success. Only you will have the specific set of obstacles and opportunities that will help define your life, so it may prove pointless to compare your level of success to that of another person.

Make a complete assessment of where you are today. It is a good idea to collaborate with someone in this analysis. A family member or a friend with similar goals as you is a good choice because they can confront you about your shortcomings and hold you accountable. It is sometimes tempting to mislead ourselves about how well we are doing, but allowing someone else to see your financial status can really stimulate you to get serious about your future. The following are a few simple questions to start the analysis:

- How much do you make today?
- Can you account for all the money you spend each month?
- How marketable are you? How many jobs are you qualified for? What would you do if you lost your current job next week?
- Do you have the skills and resources to start your own business?
- How much do you have saved? How much can you access now compared to money that is tied up in a 401k or IRA?
- How many liabilities do you have? How many things are you paying on that you do not own outright? How long will it take to pay off all your debts?
- Do you have a plan for taking care of your family in case you are unable to work or take care of your family (Disability and Life insurance)?
- How long could you make ends meet if you lost your job tomorrow? What is your backup plan?

♦ How do your expenses line up with what matters the most to you? Are you putting money into the things that you will need later in life?

Set some high level objectives that can serve as your underlying motivation. Examples would be to retire by age 50, buying your own house, owning your own successful business, getting married and having four children, or traveling to every continent at least once. After you define your highest priority objectives, put a price tag on each. Be as exact about your goals as possible, so you will know when you actually achieve them. Try to put every single goal down, even if it seems too expensive or too difficult to achieve, given your current situation. The power of a goal is not always in reaching the goal itself. It is often more powerful because it will force you to develop a plan to achieve that goal. In many cases, the journey will be more enjoyable than the destination.

Decide how often you will go through your checklist. Just like losing weight or investing, if you look for improvement every day, you may be discouraged by daily swings in progress. Typically, businesses have to file taxes quarterly or at least publish how well they did for a previous quarter. Once every three months is a good starting place to start tracking how well you are meeting your objectives.

Set intermediate goals that coincide with the regularity of your progress checks. Know that the inability to meet the small steps will ruin any chances of reaching the ultimate goal, so set goals you can achieve. Having the short-term goals also forces you to think about what it really takes to make your ultimate dreams happen.

Check the current interest rates each quarter. Make sure you are getting the best interest rates on your savings and credit accounts. Financial institutions are not obligated to keep your interest rates in line with changes that may be in your favor. As the Federal Reserve raises and lowers interest rates, the rates on your credit cards and savings/checking accounts are directly impacted. When you evaluate your financial progress, contact any financial institution with which you have an account, and inquire if you are eligible for the improved interest rates.

Principle in Action:

1. Create your baseline financial report card and leave it somewhere that will be visible to you daily.

2. Create your ultimate financial report card, as a reminder of what you are working toward.

3. Outline three steps you can take to close the gap between the ultimate scenario and your baseline.

Guiding Principle 15
Your Ideas Have Value

All of us have ideas for new business concepts or thoughts on how to improve existing products or services. However, most of us will live and die, never making any money from our original thoughts. This does not have to be the case. There are several ways to leverage your ideas to supplement your income and potentially make your mark in history.

Intellectual property (copyrights, trademarks, or patents). If you discover a new phrase, concept, invention, or visual image, you should know the steps needed to protect your discovery. A copyright is essentially the right to use a specific expression of an idea or other form of information given to you by a government agency. A trademark is a symbol or sign that a business uses to identify it or its products. A patent is the right of ownership to a certain invention, which is new and useful. For example, if you submitted and received approval for a new type of shoe that can prevent ankle sprains, you basically own all the rights to that invention and you can sell those rights to someone willing to produce and sell your invention. The process for obtaining a patent can be very time consuming and expensive, but if your patent is truly valuable, you will inevitably make your money back.

Get people interested in your idea. It's one thing to think that you have a good idea, but getting other people interested to the point that they will invest in or buy your idea is the challenge. Part of how you should present your idea is a function of what your goals are. Do you want someone to buy the idea outright, invest in you to start a company, or buy a single product from you? Take the time to understand what you really want before trying to get anyone else to take interest.

The next step is to show potential investors what customers think. Many large corporations spend a large amount of time and money placing their products in front of focus groups. Before a company will invest any production or R&D time in a project, they will make sure that there will be enough interest in the general public to justify the expense. If you have an idea, do your own field research. Show that you have tested the feasibility yourself.

Another option is to create grassroots interest. After you have protected the idea, advertise yourself. Attend conferences where the attendees would appreciate what you do. Submit papers to publications where the readers include potential investors. Be subtle in your advertising. Present your ideas in a way that show your potential to grow. The idea is to give people a reason to want to be a part of what you are doing.

Determine how much your idea is worth The value of your ideas is really a function of timing, the industry, and uniqueness of the idea. Ideally, you want to introduce ideas in an industry, where there is a large amount of investment speculation. You want to be sure that your idea is truly unique. If there are four other concepts in the market that accomplish the same objective as yours without any truly distinguishable characteristics, you are less likely to see much support. Focus less on how much the idea is worth today, but focus more on the potential value in the future. As you create and dream up new concepts and ideas, spend some time learning about the market place. Study the competition. Know what value others place on comparable items currently. Determine where the trends are going and where you fit compared to the rest of the industry. Investing is all about future return, so concentrate on telling tomorrow's story of how your idea will be successful rather than bragging about the past.

Share what you know. Write a book and share your perspective. Books have the ability to immortalize your thoughts and views like nothing else can. The greatest thing about writing books is that you can write about whatever subject matters to you. You can offer poetry, historical accounts, self-help, social commentary, or get brave and invent your own category. Although being published can be an obstacle, it is not an impossible hurdle. If a traditional publisher will not publish your book, you can save up some money and publish yourself. Make sure your voice is heard. You have a greater ability to affect others than you might think. The unique perspectives you have now are just as valuable as those you will have later in life, so don't be afraid to share your thoughts no matter how old you are.

Principle in Action:

1. Research at least two patents on something technical that you use or find fascinating. Visit the US Patent Office's website at uspto.gov. Search for the keyword, print, and read the patent.

2. Make some quiet time to write down some of your more creative ideas and research if any patents exist for those ideas. If not, seek support from peers or companies to help you file your patent.

3. Collaborate with at least one friend who respects your ideas and cultivate each other's creativity through discussion and experimentation.

Guiding Principle 16
Never Use an Easy (EZ) Return Again

Tax preparation and filing does not have to be an intimidating event. Most people file the 1040EZ form because they see it as the easy option. However, it is really the best way to make sure you overpay for taxes. The 1040EZ form does not allow you to itemize your deductions. Itemized deductions allow you to inform the government how you have spent your income to build your business, take care of your children, and support tax-deductible charities. There are numerous expenses that the federal government considers "tax deductible." However, they can only help you save money on taxes if you file the conventional 1040 form (paper or online).

Don't be afraid of filing taxes. Taxes, in an ideal world, will provide for the common infrastructure that benefits all the constituents of a given area. Tax dollars at a local level can be used to attract businesses that look for a solid location to establish themselves. Tax records on homes and income tell a story of the perceived value of an area. Businesses choose to relocate to areas based on the potential to make money in that location. If most of the businesses are cash based and never report true income values, the area appears poorer than it really is.

The key to reducing the stress of taxes is to only pay your share of the tax bill. When you spend money on things that the IRS deems deductible, you get a "write-off" or a discount on your tax bill. To be clear, write-offs are not free tickets. It simply means you do not pay taxes on the income that you used to purchase that item or service. Assume you are in the 25% tax bracket, and you made $10,000 profit from your business. The tax you would owe on that profit would be $2,500. Now, assume you spent $5,000 of that profit on expenses that you knew you would need in the next year for the business, your taxes would be $1,250 instead of $2,500. You saved on taxes, but you spent more money this year. The name of the game is spending money only on things that allow you to make more money or using your money to support non-profit organizations. Other common write-offs are charitable donations (to churches, Goodwill®, Salvation Army®), investment accounts, mortgages, and health-care costs. Your goal should be to make sure that as much of what you spend as possible falls into the tax-deductible category.

Tax returns show you and others how you manage your money. Whether you are seeking a loan or trying to establish credit, having a history of paying your taxes can go a long way. Many successful cash based businesses have a difficult time getting loans for business expansion because they do not report all their income on their tax returns. How much money you've made in the past directly affects a lender's evaluation of your credit worthiness. Trying to avoid taxes on 20% of your income is not worth the ability to get a favorable loan on a building that can increase your revenue by 100%. Here are the key things to focus on when you talk about taxes:

1. **Bigger deductions** – When you have enough itemized deductions, you will have less taxable income, which also means you pay less in taxes at the end of the day. In order to be eligible to write off deductions, you must maintain accurate accounts of what you spend. If you have a home mortgage, own a business, and/or invest into retirement savings accounts (401ks or IRAs), you are almost guaranteed to have a bigger deduction than you would if you just took the standard deduction. Maintain receipts for any expenses that help you advertise or build your business. If you have old clothes and furniture that are in usable condition, donate them to charitable organizations for a tax deduction instead of simply throwing everything away.

2. **No more big returns** – Many people see getting a large tax return as a reward. In many ways, it is the best sign that you did not plan for your tax liability optimally. The second page of the IRS's W-4 form shows you how many exemptions you can claim if you expect to write off many deductions. Remember, money has time-value. The longer you have money, the more it can be worth to you. Claiming a larger number of exemptions on your W-4 means you will have more money in your hands from each paycheck. This is money you can invest and allow to grow for you. You may end up with a smaller refund after filing taxes,

but your net profit will be higher. Consult with an accountant to determine the ideal number of exemptions for your situation.

The other trap most people fall into when they get large refunds is the desire to make large purchases as soon as the refund arrives. You will notice many companies will go out of their way to make it easy for you to spend your refund even before you get the money. If you buy things you planned for, take advantage of the special incentives that may be available to you. Please remember, the money you get back in a tax refund is not a gift. You have loaned money to the government, but you will not receive any interest in return. Your goal as a taxpayer is to claim as many exemptions as needed to break even when you file your taxes. It will require more discipline from you to save or invest the extra money you will see in each paycheck, so try not to spend what you get too quickly.

Completing a full 1040 form teaches you how to spend your money in ways that best benefit you. The tax code is set up in such a way that you receive tax breaks for investing in yourself, your business, and in the less fortunate. The basic concept is if they give you a tax break now, you will use that money to make even more money and eventually the government will receive the money they are due. You can find tax preparation software for under $20 in most stores or online that will teach you where to find deductions and file taxes.

3. **Know your tax rate schedule** – Learning how to read the tax rate schedule may help you understand the benefit of pursuing additional deductions to lower your tax bracket. For example, buying additional future supplies during the current tax year is a common practice used to manage your tax burden. Each year the tax rate can change, so it is always good to make sure you have the latest data. The first thing to do is find the table that applies to you. The choices are Single, Married filing separately, Married filing jointly (or Qualifying Widow), and Head of Household. Here is a sample 2005 tax rate schedule for single filers.

Single				
Taxable income is over	But not over	The tax is	Plus	Of the amount over
$0	$7,300	$0.00	10%	$0
7,300	29,700	730	15%	7,300
29,700	71,950	4,090.00	25%	29,700
71,950	150,150	14,652.50	28%	71,950
150,150	326,450	36,548.50	33%	150,150
326,450		94,727.50	35%	326,450

The first two columns define the lower and upper range for your tax bracket. Find the line where your taxable income falls within the ranges. Start your calculation with the corresponding tax value in the third column and add the appropriate percentage to the amount greater than the minimum value.

4. **Itemized vs. Standard Deductions** – The IRS offers standard deductions that you can take to avoid the work of itemizing your deductions. For many, the standard deductions will provide a larger break than itemizing will. However, for anyone who owns their own business, owns a house or rental property, or gives to charity among other things, itemizing can quickly reduce how much you owe in taxes.

Exemption/deductions	2004	2005	2006
Personal exemptions	$3,100	$3,200	$3,300
Standard deduction			
Married Filed Joint	9,700	10,000	13,000
Head of Household	7,500	7,300	7,550
Single or Separate	4,800	5,000	5,150
Child tax exemption	800	800	850

5. **Avoid underpayment penalties** – If you own a business or receive income that is not regularly taxed with each payment, you are required to file quarterly taxes. Every three months, you will send the IRS a check for the estimated tax liability for that period. The S-4 form comes with a workbook to help you understand how much you would owe. Not paying these taxes can result in underpayment penalties that are assessed each quarter. These penalties can grow rapidly.

Principle in Action:

1. Get copies of the 1040 and the 1040 EZ tax booklets and spend a few hours skimming the contents.

2. Locate a local organization or tax preparation company that offers training and take the class. Not only will it help you prepare your own taxes, but it will also allow you to make extra money during tax season.

3. Calculate what percentage of your income you have paid in taxes in the past.

4. Investigate what "write-offs" you are eligible for.

5. Attend at least one local political event where the use of your tax money is discussed so that you learn how your tax dollars are spent.

Niche

Before you attempt to take on the world, learn from and better your immediate sphere of influence.

Guiding Principle 17
Maximize Exposure to the Experienced

Making and preserving money is not just about hard work. Often it is about avoiding the pitfalls that are not obvious and being prepared to take advantage of opportunities when they arise. Experience is usually the best teacher, but since there are only so many hours in a day, there is no way you can experience everything. You need access to people with more expertise than you have. The goal is to learn, but remember that you have something to offer too. You have experiences and perspective that the people you meet could never have. As you share of yourself, others will be more inclined to reciprocate the giving. Business is not a charity, so always come to the table with something. Consider these options for associating with people who have proven to be successful.

Network within your organization or company. Get a copy of your company's organizational chart(s). Pursue lunch meetings with those who are where you want to be. Most people enjoy the opportunity to help another person grow, as long as it does not get in the way of their own personal agenda. Locate where your position fits within the company. If your company has national or global reach, look beyond just your local office's management team. Dealing with the grind of a "9 to 5" job is made more manageable if you have in mind something more than just getting paid each week. You should not rely exclusively on your company to develop a meaningful career path for you. It is YOUR career, and it will ultimately grow based on where you want it to go. As you meet more people in different areas, you get a better sense of where you do or do not want your career to go.

Network within your trade or field. Seek out all the magazines, newsletters, and clubs dedicated to that thing that you ultimately want to do professionally. There is a club for just about anything you could imagine. Scan local colleges for lecture series by prominent professionals in your area of interest. Although the internet gives a lot of useful information, there is still no substitute for dedicated trade magazines. They tell you the most about upcoming events, job opportunities, and changes/trends in the industry. Subscribe to at least one such magazine and attend local trade events. Even if you are significantly younger or less experienced than the core group of members, continue to participate. Your goal is knowledge transfer. If the group has a conference and the cost is too high, write in as a prospective member who is interested in attending part of the conference. Ask for a one-day pass. The worst they can do is say no. However, if you present a case for how you can add value to their organization, you may receive a guest pass.

Attend formal and charitable events. Attend anything from banquets to picnics and charity sporting events to community clean-up days. Look for events held by the groups that are associated with your areas of interest. Most professional groups have social events on their calendars. Most of the social events are not open to the public, so you may have to join the group just to attend functions. The charitable outreach programs and volunteer opportunities may be the best way to show someone what kind of person you are. Planned social events tend to be restrictive, so it is difficult to create meaningful connections. However, serving side by side at a food bank or a children's hospital can create memories and bonds that will last.

Principle in Action:

1. Evaluate your circle of friends/peers and count how many of them have done the things you want to do or even aspire to similar goals.

2. Make the effort to enter new circles where you can meet and associate with people who have similar goals as you.

Guiding Principle 18
Follow the Money Trail

A good way to build your financial awareness is to study how those in your immediate community and people around the world spend money. Even with your own money, look at how many people benefit from each dollar you spend. Many successful businesses make money by offering products and services in areas where people are already spending money. Other companies become successful by studying how other businesses spend money. Having businesses as your end customer can prove to be very lucrative. When you buy an item, consider why the price is what it is, and you may discover your next business opportunity. When you see a successful person, consider all the places he or she spends their money. It may sound strange, but I even want you study spending habits in bad times. Investigate what you need to recover from the losses and put yourself in a position to fill those needs.

What are the components of price? Break down what goes into producing and delivering the products you use. You are likely to find ways to save and/or make more money. For example, if you are buying a product that weighs over 100 pounds, consider that a part of the retail cost includes some of the shipping costs that the manufacturer or retailer is absorbing. So, if you live close to the company's warehouse or distribution center, you may be able to save money by picking it up yourself. The simplest case that most people can take advantage of is the delivery costs associated with furniture or appliances. If you do not have a truck, keep the number of a friend who does. You can treat him or her to a free meal or a tank of gas as repayment. You will save significantly on what you would pay the retailer for delivery. Another option is to rent a truck if you have multiple items to transport.

As you begin to understand why the things you buy cost as much as they do, you will see more areas where you can provide services or discover jobs that you have never considered before. Let's examine all the jobs that are associated with each box of cereal you buy. Since, most cereals have some form of grain (oats, wheat, barley, etc), we will start the chain with Farmers. Note that there really is no perfect place to start this analysis since dependencies exist between all industries. For example, farmers are supported by an entire industry of farming equipment, fertilizers, pesticides, and other services. In addition, a whole industry is built around producing the milk needed for your cereal, which we will not touch in this example. The FARMER sells his grain to a cereal maker, who will likely pay a TRUCKING company to transport the raw material to a processing center. Depending on the time of the year, some type of STORAGE facility may be required. MANUFACTURERS provide equipment to process the raw material into the cereal.

Each cereal company has RESEARCH AND DEVELOPMENT organizations that are constantly working to make a better, cheaper, and more appealing product. A PLASTICS company provides the bags or material for the bags that will hold the cereal. A PAPER products company will create the boxes that hold the bags. A MARKETING company will devise the branding and aesthetic components of the box cover. A SALES team will determine the best promotions to use to get the product sold quickly. That sales team will have to travel extensively to meet potential buyers and retailers to buy the product. A DISTRIBUTION company will be involved in storing and delivering the products to the GROCERY STORE that will sell the products.

Each link in the chain accounts for part of the cost of the cereal you buy. One reason why generic brand cereals can sell the similar products cheaper is that they cut out some steps. Some do not have boxes for their cereal (just bags), and they do not have to worry nearly as much about sales and marketing. They may just use the name of the grocery store as their brand. As you research more products, look for places where you could start a business or help an existing business improve their process. There are also opportunities for you to create your own company, provide a competing service, or better yet help one of the existing companies make or save more money. If your methods and services are unique, you could potentially serve all the competitors and multiply your earning power.

Where do the wealthy spend their money? Another productive activity is devoting some time to learning where people in the higher income brackets spend their money. You may be surprised to see that many of them are discrete with how they spend money. For the most part, these people work more than 40 hours a week. As they devote more time to the business of making money, they may not have as much time to do things for themselves. Simple things like cooking, running errands, lawn care, home maintenance and cleaning, among other services are all possible avenues for making money from those who make the most money.

Understand the demographic of the wealthy and consider what matters the most to them. Are the wealthy people in your area young? Do they still have children a home? Are you in a metropolitan area or rural area? All these factors will tell you what types of business have the most marketability. It is much harder to convince people they need your business than it is to find out where they already have a need and fill that.

Where is the most money spent during the worst times? When there is a disaster, a war, or an economic down period, new millionaires are born. It may sound borderline unethical to profit from someone's misfortune, but the reality is many large companies exist because they were able to provide assistance when people needed it the most. My hope is that you will enter such opportunities with fairness in mind as you meet the needs of those who are struggling. At the same time, you can build institutions that will serve that community for years to come. Businesses cannot be charities, but charities should be run as businesses. The primary goal of a business is to make money. Therefore, many do great things for their community. As a business, you need income to stay in existence, so make sure you protect your bottom line even when your heart makes it difficult. Charities fill a role in a community as do businesses. Try to keep the differences clear.

Principle in Action:

1. Find at least two household items that you can lay out the money trail for. Try to identify every link in the chain from raw materials to production to distribution.
2. Identify what part of the trail is the most interesting to you and presents a possible career path.

Guiding Principle 19
Start Your Own Businesses

Starting a business is one of the best ways to apply what you have learned about managing money, and you will learn new lessons along the way that will help you in your every day life. Too often, people think the primary goal of running a business is just to make as much money as possible. However, at the end of the day, it is really about how much of the money you are able to keep. Making $1,000,000 every year is not very impressive if the business spends $1,000,000 every year. If a competitor only makes $500,000, but spends $300,000, they are the more successful company.

Although, the recommendation is that you start your own business as soon as you are able, I will always caution that you grow your business at a rate where your revenue growth always exceeds your expenses. In many cases, you can start your business even while you maintain your "day job." You may have to sacrifice much of your free time, but you will significantly decrease the risk involved in starting your business. Because most people see a business as a storefront or a product, they focus most of their energy and resources on just getting started. The assumption is, "if I build it they will come." Unfortunately, most small businesses fail because they spend too much too soon. As a result, the company runs out of money before they can make the revenue they anticipated. In many cases, starting a business does not mean you have to spend any money. When you start a business, do as much as you can to get a head start. Spend extra time doing market research to understand your customers, their spending patterns, and their loyalty to one brand. Become an expert on anything that could affect how much money you might make.

You do not have to get thousands of dollars in loans. If you are patient and disciplined, you can often start a small successful business that can fuel its own growth. In other words, you grow as fast as your past successes lets you grow. If you decide to take out a loan, force yourself to predict how much each dollar you borrow will make for you later. There is no such thing as free money. Money makes more money. It is very tempting to enter business with the visions of making millions, and my hope is that you will. However, each million starts with the first few dollars. If you can effectively manage your cash flow when your income is low, the same habits will allow you to grow your earnings faster as your revenue increases.

Many small businesses fail in the first three years, often because the business owner never planned for the worst case. Most business plans target idealistic goals, without enough thought for building safety nets. The best-case goals can keep you motivated and inspire others to support and follow you. The safety nets allow you to stay around long enough to see your goals achieved. In the early days of forming your business, put together a plan for yourself. Write it as if the wealthiest person in the world might read it to consider giving you a loan. What would they want to see to persuade them that this would be a good investment? Does the business have a clear objective? Does the business have a clear potential customer base? Is the business aware of its weaknesses (internal and against competition)? Does the business have a plan for growth and paying back debt? As you read about the legal entities, try to think about why some businesses may make more sense as a sole proprietorship instead of a partnership, a corporation instead of a sole proprietorship, etc.

There are entire books written about how to create a business plan, so it is unlikely you'll find one method that works for every type of business. One of the best ways to create a business plan is to mimic the plan of a successful business in your field. As you research all the risks and rewards of your potential business, make sure you develop relationships with successful entrepreneurs. Ask them for samples of their first business plans and find out what they would do differently if they had to start a new business today.

Sole Proprietorship – A sole proprietorship is a business where the owner is an individual. This means you get all the profits and risks. Every dollar you make after paying expenses and taxes is yours to keep. At the same time, if you get into financial or legal trouble, your personal property (house, cars, jewelry, etc) could be seized to pay off the company's debts. Sole proprietorships can have zero start-up costs. For example, you can start a lawn care company tomorrow as a sole proprietor at no cost if you already have equipment. If cooking is your talent, you can easily turn your passion into a business that brings in extra revenue.

The key with Sole Proprietorships is to minimize your risk and expenses. Debt is one of the most powerful forces of financial momentum. The more debt you have, the harder it is to get out of debt. Although it is a slower way to grow a company, self-funding is a popular option among sole proprietors. Many will save for years before starting the business; others will live from what they make month to month from their business. Both options have pros and cons depending on the type of business and your expected revenue schedule. A business that depends on manufacturing or long lead times would tend to need larger cash reserves than a company that receives payment as service is delivered. If you sell to big companies, expect payment according to their schedules. The budgetary cycles and processes of large corporations often cost the small companies on a daily basis. The bigger companies tend to pay their bills on their own schedule, not necessarily when you bill them. As a small business, you cannot celebrate too much during the good times because the slow periods can be very difficult. Spread out your expenses, even when you have extra money in the bank.

Partnerships – A partnership differs from sole proprietorship in that a sole proprietor has total control and partnerships involve the agreement of two or more people to form a business together. The members of the partnership will share the risk and rewards. Similar to a sole proprietorship, you can create a partnership without extensive local or state paperwork. Too often though, people define partnerships very loosely, relying on verbal agreements. Friends usually make bad business partners because they assume too much, about what the other person will do. When times are going well, partnerships work great, however, when challenges arise, the weaknesses in the partnership model are exposed. If one partner makes a catastrophic mistake that gets the company in trouble, all partners are equally liable. If one partner does not agree with something or is not pulling their weight, it can become very difficult to keep the business running efficiently.

When it comes to business, try to minimize informal arrangements. Understanding and cooperation erodes when times get hard, and you will need some hard rules or organizational hierarchy to fall back on. Someone has to be the boss. Obviously, there will be exceptions, but be prepared for conflicts when they arise. From major corporations to local community shops, mergers and partnerships fail regularly. The fundamental problem occurs because the two parities enter the arrangement assuming they can continue with "business as usual." However, it is rare that any two people or groups will have the exact same objectives and approaches to getting things done. At the end of the day, one person has to be the boss (the person who will have the final vote). Both parties have to be prepared to compromise.

If you decide to pursue a partnership, establish some rules that all partners agree to sign off on. The following are a few things to consider:

◆ Chain of Command – Even in a partnership, it is advisable that one person have the final say so. It is very difficult to manage all decisions by committee.

◆ Risk/Reward Divisions – If the partnership is a true 50/50 arrangement, spell it out in a document. Many times, one person may put up more money to start the company and will in turn assume that they deserve a larger payout or greater decision-making power. Never make assumptions about payment distribution, decision-making rules, or any other business practices. Spell it out. Sign on it.

◆ Long term Objective of the company – Be sure that all partners sit down and discuss their long-term vision for the company. If one of you wants to grow the company as quickly as possible and try to sell it to the first bidder, but the other one wants to develop a business he can leave to his children, then you have a problem. Many partnerships dissolve because of these types of issues, even when the business is doing well. Choose your partners carefully.

Corporations – People form corporations to limit liability or allow shareholders to participate in the ownership of a company. Starting a corporation usually requires more paperwork and fees to get the company off the ground than the other options. The concept of limited liability means that if the company gets in trouble (default on loans or faces law suits), only the company's assets are liable. In a sole proprietorship or partnership, the personal property of the business owners is at risk for the payment of the company's debts or liabilities.

There are three types of corporations: C Corporation, S Corporation, and LLC (Limited Liability Company). The type that is best for you really depends on the type of company you are creating and the goals of that company. It is worth the money to sit with an accountant and/or lawyer to discuss your options (that expense is deductible). Ask questions about how each business entity is taxed, the impact of double taxation (will the company and the individuals both pay taxes on earnings distributed as dividends), and the rules to start and maintain each type of corporation. There is usually a state filing fee involved with forming a corporation. A corporation may not be the best option for someone who wants total control over all decisions. However, it is usually easier to raise money as a corporation, because investors become legal shareholders.

Principle in Action:

1. Identify three types of businesses that you could start if you had access to as much money as you needed.

2. Identify what type of business model best fits your business and your long term goals

3. Write a business plan for yourself that can evolve into something that you could give to a bank or investor to help finance your business.

Self-Improvement
Dedicate yourself to a lifestyle of constant self-improvement. Each day look for ways to become better at something than you were the day before.

Guiding Principle 20
Be Accountable for Your Own Financial Health

You don't have to be an expert in all areas, but you should know enough to make informed decisions. The tough question is what is enough? The goal should be to know enough to make sure that you know when someone is misleading you. You want to know when you are overpaying for something. You also want to stay informed about as many topics as possible so that you can take advantage of opportunities when they are available.

One of the best ways to make money is to find something that you are good at (preferably something that most people do not want to do) and charge for your services. Many of the services you pay for work on this principle. In general, you pay them whatever they ask because it is just not worth the headache to do it yourself. When it comes to your investing your money, you want to be a bit more careful. Before you give someone significant control of how your money is managed, learn as much as you can so that you can understand and challenge the decisions that are made for you.

Learn how to budget your own home/business finances. However, a budget is only useful if you use it. It takes time and discipline to follow a budget, but it is the best thing you can do to maintain financial stability. Even if you can just start with a list of all your regular monthly expenses, you are ahead of most people. Consider breaking up your spending into general categories, where it is clear what you can be flexible with when times get difficult. An example might be:

♦ Mandatory Expenses – any expense you have to pay to avoid penalty. These nonflexible expenses include rent/mortgage, food, utilities (cable, phone, electric, gas, water, etc), groceries, loans/credit cards (minimum payments plus enough extra on the principle to pay off the loan quickly), car (gasoline, insurance, and maintenance).

♦ Flexible Expenses – any expense associated with leisure and entertainment. These flexible expenses include entertainment (movies, CDs, DVDs, clubs, bars), eating out (especially lunch at work), and clothing. Perhaps the most difficult battle is in how you prioritize and are able to control your flexible expenses. Money spent here is usually what keeps people from being able to control their budgets.

♦ Long-term planning expenses – anything that you put money towards that you will require waiting several months or years before you can realize the value of your investment. Some examples include savings account, retirement accounts, saving for down payments or large purchases (furniture, vacations).

Determine the Mandatory Expenses first, so that you know how much to budget for your flexible expenses. If possible, withdraw the budgeted flexible expense amount in cash at the beginning of each month. For most people, it is easier to spend $100 on a credit card or debit card than to give up the same amount in cash.

Develop your own retirement plan. Many people think it takes becoming a millionaire to be able to retire comfortably. For most people that is far from true. The magic number is a function of how many recurring expenses you have, how old you are when you retire, and what kind of income (pensions, annuities, social security, or part-time jobs) you have coming in after retirement. In addition, for a growing number of people, retirement just means leaving a traditional 9 to 5 job. Many "retired" people continue to work part time jobs or find other ways to keep income flowing in. The sooner you start preparing for retirement, the easier the process will be.

Learn to do your own taxes. Even if you pay an accountant to do your taxes, you still have to sign off on what they prepare. It is important for you to understand what you are signing. As an added benefit, knowing the way the tax code is written will help you learn the best ways to spend and grow money effectively. Several software applications take you through the steps of tax preparation. Many of them will actually give you tips on how to lower your tax bill for future years. If you keep receipts and records of your spending, anyone can spend a few hours and complete their taxes without much difficulty.

Learn how to buy and sell your own stocks. Get a brokerage account so you can have the option to invest on your own and have access to research tools. Even if you invest in mutual funds or 401ks, empower yourself by researching the companies that your money is financing. One of the good things about the "day trading" boom of the late 90's is that it made it easier for the average person to invest directly in the stock market, without paying a licensed broker or firm large commissions. Today, you can buy or sell stock for less than a $10 commission. Be careful of companies that will charge you an additional fee for the number of shares you sell. That can become very costly if you invest in less expensive stocks.

Even if you do not feel comfortable buying and selling your own shares, these brokerage accounts often come with many free tools that can help you monitor how your mutual funds or stocks are performing. If someone is managing your money, you have every right and obligation to ask questions and seek justification for decisions that they are making. If you have a mutual fund composed of five stocks, add them to some kind of watch list, where you are able to keep up with news, price, and analyst coverage on those stocks. If all the signs are negative about a stock, make the broker tell you why he keeps investing your money into something that appears to be heading in the wrong direction. Look for new opportunities in your personal life too. If you are happy with a new product and the company has great potential to grow, notify your broker and determine if the stock is a good place to put some of your money. New opportunities become available daily, so don't lose sleep about missed opportunities.

Although, your suggestions and questions may irritate some brokers and financial planners, a good one will listen to you and give you sound reasons for the decisions that he or she is making.

Principle in Action:

1. Identify two areas where you are relying totally on someone else's expertise to take care of your best interests.

2. Set up a meeting where you can ask that person or company questions about how and why they make the investment decisions that they do.

3. Find at least one area where you will plan to take on more responsibility.

Guiding Principle 21
Some Deals ARE Too Good to be True

This principle does not mean that you always have to buy the most expensive option all the time, but in the back of your mind, start to consider how much each purchase will cost you in the end. Become critical of anything that costs significantly less than the rest of the competition. Learning to have the discipline to look at the total cost and not just the immediate cost can save you tremendously over time. The following are a few common examples of very expensive cheap purchases.

Cheap Cars - Whenever you buy a used car, always ask the seller why they are selling the car, and correlate that with your own instincts and logic. In many cases, you are receiving a car with some known maintenance problem that the owner did not want to fix. Ask for maintenance records. Don't pay as much for a car that does not come with maintenance records. Look for evidence of any engine problems or examples of repairs that appear several times. Find out the last time the owner replaced brakes and tires. Use a company that can perform a background check for cars. They will let you know if the car has been in any accidents or incurred any major damage, like flooding. You don't want to buy a $1000 car if you have to put in $2000 of work from the beginning. You would be better off buying a newer more stable $3000 car.

Rent To Own – Be very careful about renting to own appliances and furniture. As with anything, there are cases where this may make more sense, but in general, it will cost you more in the long term than it will save you. The attraction to these offers is the low monthly payments and the ability to have what you want now. The problem is you can quickly pay more than the item is worth. If you can have the patience to wait and save a few months or buy from a store that offers you a no interest or deferred interest option, you will usually come out better.

Deferred Interest – Consider the 12 month same as cash options or 18 months with no interest payment offers only if you can afford to pay off the full amount in the time given. Otherwise, the cost of the purchase can increase dramatically when the unpaid interest accrues. It is not a good idea to assume that you will have money when the payment term comes due, unless you are saving money towards that final payment. Ideally, seek out interest-free payment options because you can also invest what you are saving on interest in a short-term safe investment option, like a savings account or a money market account.

Low Lease Payments – The longer you are willing to stay in a lease, the lower the monthly rate the seller will offer. The longer you hold on to a leased item, the closer you get to the line where it would have made more sense to buy the item. Remember, for as long as you lease something, you really are just paying for the right to use it. So, if you decide to buy it at the end of the lease, you will have overpaid.

"Low Price" Advertisements – Sometimes the price can be too low. Companies have to make their money somewhere, either through maintenance costs, add-ons, or referrals. Trust your instincts when the price appears to be too good to be true. Companies that are not profitable don't last. So you could get a great deal now, but be stuck with an unsupported product later.

Principle in Action:

1. Find two items or industries where it is clear that paying less now will hurt you in the end.

2. Visit a car dealership and have them provide you the costs for leasing a car and buying the same car. Calculate the costs over the terms for both scenarios.

Guiding Principle 22
Know How to Get Answers

There is no shame in admitting that you do not know everything. A smart person is very aware of their weaknesses and limitations. The key is to have a way to get information or assistance when you need it. For example, you could read every line of tax code or you can develop a friendship with a tax accountant who can answer questions for you. Here are a few resources you can also cultivate:

Library – Libraries are great for many reasons. If for no other reason, go to your local library to find a quiet place to get away from your daily distractions. It is a place where your mind can slow down enough to process information. Libraries offer free access to books in all areas imaginable. They usually also offer free internet access. You can read current and past periodicals (magazines and newspapers) from all over the world. In all honesty, libraries are not free. Part of your state and local taxes pay for the building and maintenance of libraries, so you might as well get what you pay for. Many libraries offer special programs for children and adults that can accelerate your exposure to new material.

If you are studying an academic subject or a task that is causing you difficulties at work, there is usually a book that can provide you additional insight on how to interpret the information. The internet is incredible for allowing you to keep up with current events, but sometimes, the sheer volume of information makes it hard to get a complete body of work on a specific topic. Make time to visit your local library at least once a month for a couple of hours. Read something in an area you currently know nothing about. Pick up a magazine or newspaper from another part of the country or world. Inevitably, you will learn something that you can use to improve your quality of life.

Internet – The Internet is called the "Information Superhighway" for a good reason. With a few clicks, you can begin learning about almost anything very quickly. You can search a keyword or phrase and a search engine will return several sites with the information you are seeking. The challenge is really in being able to process that information so that you can use it. A few sites are trying to do that. Two sites attempt to consolidate useful data are Wikipedia.com and Investopedia.com. As with anything you read, watch, or find on the web, try to verify the sources before you believe what you see. Look for multiple reputable sources before accepting information as fact. Many internet search engines offer access to specialized groups. People with a particular interest in a specific area usually subscribe to these groups. In these groups, you can get the perspectives and experiences of people from all over the world. You can ask questions in a group and have them answered by several people in that internet group.

Peers in other industries – As you mature, relationships tend to become more functional in many ways. One benefit in maintaining many friendships with people who are in different industries than you is that you always have a direct path to new sources of information. Two people from different backgrounds can look at the same problem and derive two completely different solutions. Your friends and peers can have far more value than just socializing. Find out where they are experts, and let them know about your unique experiences. Talk about more than sports and the weather. Together, you could create businesses that no one else could.

Previous generations – Ask someone with a little more experience than you have. Everyone likes to feel useful, and teaching youth makes almost anybody feel a sense of accomplishment. One of life's dilemmas is reaching the end of your life to find out that you have no one to pass your knowledge and experience to. Sadly, this happens every day. Most young people do not understand the value of an older person's wisdom until they have gone through their share of bad experiences. Listen. It may save you a lot of pain and accelerate your path toward your ultimate success.

Principle in Action:

1. Get a library card and check out a book about the career that you find the most interesting.

2. Set aside time to find out what your friends do on their jobs. Make time to share/discuss your expertise with them.

Guiding Principle 23
Raise Your Financial IQ

Regardless of what industry you choose to go into, your ability to speak the language of finance will distinguish you from your peers who are just happy to have a job. The ability to understand balance sheets, income statements, and cash flow statements will propel your personal finances and make you a vital member of any company. There is no way I can do this subject justice in the few pages before you, but I hope to get you started with something you can build upon. Half of the battle is knowing what questions to ask and what information you should spend more time researching

Be able to read a Balance Sheet – A balance sheet gives a statement of the financial position of a company at a given point in time. They are usually prepared quarterly and annually. The primary theme of the balance sheet is that the assets should equal to the total liabilities plus the shareholder equity.

♦ Asset – essentially everything a company owns. Some assets are things that actively change hands such as cash, inventory, and accounts receivable. Other assets are considered fixed such as buildings, land, and equipment.

♦ Liabilities – anything that a company owes. In general, current liabilities are due within the fiscal year, such as taxes and wages. Long-term liabilities are those that are due in more than one year, such as debt that has a three-year maturity.

♦ Shareholder Equity – the net worth of the company. This is a function of the investment in the company and the accumulated profits after any dividends are paid.

Be able to read an Income Statement – The purpose of an income statement is to show a company's earnings for a specified period. Stated another way, the income statement shows net income by calculating the difference between the total revenue and the total expenses for any period.

♦ Total Revenue – the total money brought in from the sale of goods and services.

♦ Cost of Revenue – the cost of doing business and the cost of producing the things you sell.

♦ Gross Profit – the difference between the total revenue and the cost of revenue.

♦ Selling, General, and Administrative – the cost of getting your goods and services to market and paying for the employees you have.

Be able to read a Cash Flow Statement – The purpose of the cash flow statement is to show the actual cash that a company brings in and spends during a specific period of time. A cash flow statement tells a story about a company's ability to manage money. If you ever need to borrow money, the ability to show how you manage cash will go a long way in securing a loan. As with the other statements, cash flow can easily become very complicated. The key elements are:

♦ Cash from Operating Activities – the amount of money spent to perform the functions of the business subtracted from the revenue that the business brought in directly from operating the business.

♦ Cash from Investing Activities – the amount of money gained or lost from investments that the company has made.

♦ Cash from Financing Activities – the cash received or paid in transactions that involve borrowing or selling equity in the company.

Pay attention to Margins - The heart of most money management is understanding margins. It does not matter how much you make if you spend more than you make. You can be a great success and only sell one item, if that one item costs you significantly less to make than you sold it for. Consider the case of spending $50,000 to renovate a $200,000 house that later sells for $400,000. You can also be successful if you sell items for a few pennies over cost if you are able to sell millions of them. A margin is the difference between how much something costs you and what you get in return when you sell the item. If you understand margins, you will make decisions that people who only think of the actual dollar amount will never understand. Mathematically, calculating margins is a matter of doing some subtraction and applying what you have learned about percentages. If you can maintain predictable margins, you will be ahead of the game in most areas.

If it costs me $4 to design/build/distribute a toy and I sell it for $5, I am making $1 for each toy I sell. One dollar divided by $5 means that I am getting a 20% margin. If another person spends the same as me to get a toy sold, but decides to sell his toy for $10, he will achieve $6 per toy and achieve a 60% margin. To make the first million dollars, I have to sell one million toys, while the other person only has to sell 170,000 toys. The reality of the marketplace, however, will usually dictate that the person who will buy the $10 toy instead of the $5 toy will expect more, so the cost to produce the $10 toy will go up and his margins will go down. Entire industries live and die by their ability to understand how to price. You cannot understand how to price if you do not understand your costs and then set your desired margin. For most people/businesses, the ability to achieve the highest margin possible is the primary goal, but it is a delicate balance of how well you can control your costs and how much you earn from your products.

Know why the Federal Reserve matters - As you have read in many of these financial guiding principles, the importance of interest rates continues to show up frequently. The impact of debt on your life and the ability to grow wealth for most people is directly tied to interest rates. In the US, the Federal Reserve sets the countries monetary policy. Part of doing that is setting the prime interest rate or the rate at which banks borrow money from each other. The prime rate serves as a foundation for the interest rate that other institutions will lend money and the rate that they will offer to those who invest in them. You do not have to become a financial expert to appreciate the decisions made by the Federal Reserve. When interest rates are relatively low, it makes more sense to borrow money than when they are higher. If the prime rate is low, your credit card company can often offer you a lower rate. If you already have a house on a 30 year fixed rate that is higher than the current rate, you may also refinance your home at the lower interest rate and save yourself some money.

When interest rates are high, you will want to invest more of your money into stable savings accounts, CDs, or Bonds. You do not have to carry so much of the risk involved in stocks when the long-term interest rates provide you comparable returns on low risk investment options. There are few financial plans that work for all situations. A smart investor can take advantage of changes in the environment to make the most with his/her money.

Principle in Action:

1. Purchase or check out an accounting book that has sample problems with accompanying answers.

2. Set aside an hour per week to watch a financial news network show. Try to get familiar with the language they use.

Guiding Principle 24
You Always Have Options

Making sound financial decisions increases the number of options you will have. With careful planning and the willingness to take advantage of each opportunity presented, every person can begin to control their own financial future. Sometimes, it just boils down to having the courage to change. Either you change the way you look at things or you change your habits. The fear of change is paralyzing and in most cases, the things we fear never happen. If the change does not work, you can always go back to what was comfortable.

Feeling as if you have no choice gives you an excuse to accept whatever is handed to you. Your starting place in life will be different from everyone else's. The obstacles you will encounter and overcome will be unique, but no matter how tough the road ahead may look, YOU ALWAYS HAVE OPTIONS!

I am not much of a cheerleader, but I understand the value of feeling good about yourself and your future. Remember the keywords that I have associated with the word OPTIONS. No matter what people say and no matter how you feel, YOU ALWAYS HAVE OPTIONS:

Opportunity – Keep your eyes open, there is always more money to be made. Sometimes you have to make an opportunity, so don't wait for it to fall from the sky.

Plan – Having a plan for how you will make and spend money is a powerful tool by itself. It will force you to prioritize and set goals. Research, write, and work your plan. Success is unavoidable.

Tools – Tools simply allow you to complete a task in a more effective or productive way than you could without the tool. Equip yourself with as many financial tools as possible so that you are prepared for the tasks you will face.

Interest – Understanding how to grow your money with interest, while minimizing the interest on your debts is what separates those who just make money from those who are wealthy.

Originality – There is only one you, and by default, that makes you original. You don't have to follow anyone's path or mold. Try to develop your own perspectives about spending and saving money. Listen to others, pull out the best from what you hear, but chart your own path and stick to it.

Niche – There is a combination of people and businesses that only you interact with. You can connect the dots in ways that no one else can. Use the resources that are available to you to create new solutions. Master what you can control before venturing out into uncharted waters.

Self-improvement – No matter how much experience and talent you have, keep fine-tuning your skills and learning new concepts and ways of doing things. What worked for you yesterday may not be sufficient for the next task. Keep learning, trying new things, and challenging what you define as normal. There is no limit to what you can do.

If you still don't think you have options, go back to the first page or use your creativity to define your own options.

Principle in Action:

1. Wake up every morning and remind yourself, "I Always Have Options." Look for new ways to make, spend, and save money each day. That's it. Try it for two weeks and see how your approach to life begins to change.

Glossary

Accrue – to accumulate over time; usually associated with interest payments. If a lender offers delayed payments or no-interest payment plans, they typically will allow the interest costs to **accrue**. If you do not pay back the full amount due, on time, you will be charged all the accrued interest in addition to the principal you owe.

Annuity – an agreement or contract typically sold by insurance companies that pays the recipient at regularly scheduled intervals and for a set period. Annuities are usually a retirement tool to help retirees establish a fixed or predictable income flow.

Assets – anything that has value that you can use to obtain something else of value. In your personal finances, assets include investments in savings accounts, retirement accounts, houses, and cars (most cars lose value with time).

Broker – person who acts as a middleman for various types of financial transactions such as real-estate purchases, insurance, stocks, and bonds. Most brokerage relationships involve commissions. Consumers should compare the differences between the commissions and services associated with each broker before choosing one.

Budget – a financial plan based on expected revenue and expenses for a set period. Actual income and spending should be reviewed frequently and compared with what was budgeted, and adjustments should be made accordingly.

Charity – organization established to provide products or services to those who need assistance. The U.S. tax code provides for tax deductions for donations made to charitable organizations.

Commissions – financial compensation package awarded to a person or organization that sells a product or service. As a consumer, always verify advice given from a person who receives a commission to make sure that the advice is in your best interest.

Deductions - expenses that are recognized by the Internal Revenue Service (IRS), which reduce your taxable income. The amount of income tax you owe is not based on your total income, but rather on the difference between your total income and your deductible expenses (also known as a "Tax Write-Off").

Deferment – the ability to delay repayment associated with various payment plans. Deferment is typically more of a short-term relief than a long-term solution. When deferred payments are due, they usually come with hefty accrued interest payments. If you take advantage of deferment, use the grace period to save money that will be used towards repayment.

Diluting – the process of reducing the value of an asset or investment. Stocks often are diluted when the company issues additional shares of stock to finance operations. In general, the more available something is, the more diluted or less valuable it is.

Diversification – the act of spreading investment dollars into different areas to reduce risk. Investors who place all their money into one specific stock or type of investment are completely dependent on the performance of that one stock. A diversified portfolio attempts to combine investments that have different growth patterns and risk profiles.

Dividends – the way management shares earnings with the owners of the company (shareholders). You can become a shareholder by receiving stock as a gift or as payment for services you provide, or you can buy shares of stock if the company is publicly traded. Dividends can be paid in many forms including money or more stock.

Entrepreneur – a person who starts a business. The challenges involved with being an entrepreneur include raising enough money to start the company and generating consistent income. The benefits include the ability to have more control of how much you make and how much you work.

Equity – when used in investing, equity refers to the amount of ownership a person has in a company. With respect to loans and property, equity is the difference between how much something is worth and the outstanding debt.

Finance – (used as a verb in this book) refers to a method of paying for expenses by using some type of payment plan. Most plans involve payment terms, interest, and/or additional late penalties. An ideal financing plan offers a 0% interest rate, long repayment periods, and no penalties, like accrued interest if the loan is not paid in full by the end of the repayment period. If you choose to finance a purchase, pay attention to the terms.

Mutual Fund – a collection of stocks, bonds, or other investment options that are managed by a person or company.

Inflation – the process by which prices go up as products become less available. As the economy grows, some inflation is expected. If inflation grows too fast, consumers have difficulty purchasing products and the economy slows down, impacting jobs and wages. As you forecast future expenses and income, always consider the impact of inflation. Something that costs $100 today could easily cost $200 in 15 years because of inflation.

Insurance – arrangement where a person or company pays another person or company a premium to provide financial protection from trouble. Some examples of common insurance are automobile, health, home, and life. Each provides the benefits in correspondence to the amount of insurance purchased.

Invest (investment) – the act of using money or any other capital to make more money. Investment growth is a function of risk and time. Higher risk investments tend to have shorter expected return periods, while low risk investments are used to generate consistent income over longer periods.

Leasing – paying for use of an object instead of paying to own that object. Renting an apartment or home is often called leasing. Leasing can be a good short-term option for automobiles and homes. However, over the long term, leases tend to cost the consumer more than a standard purchase.

Liability – in the simplest terms, a liability is anything that you do not completely own. If you are in the third year of a 5-year car loan, the remaining principle on the car loan is recorded as a liability.

Liquid (assets) – the ability to access money quickly, with cash or the sale other assets in a timely manner without incurring excessive penalties.

Margins – the difference between what it costs to design, build, and deliver a product or service and how much that product or service is sold for.

Mortgage – an agreement between a borrower and a lender, where the lender buys a property for a borrower and has a right to take ownership of a property if the borrower does not meet their obligation. Mortgages are typically characterized by long-term loans.

Net Worth – the difference between assets and liabilities. Assets include equity in homes, investments, and cash. Liabilities include home loans or any other unpaid debt. You do not have to have a million dollar salary to become a millionaire; you can amass millions in assets over time.

Pensions – funds set up by many companies or other organizations for providing employees with a salary after retirement. When companies struggle economically, pensions are sometimes reduced or eliminated. As you plan for retirement, try to make sure that you do not rely exclusively on pension income.

Retire (retirement) – the point at which a person stops or reduces work and starts to live off the income generated by previous investments or pensions. As you work toward retirement, remember that the more you can make or invest early, the sooner you will be able to retire.

Shareholders – anyone who owns at least one share of stock in a company. Stock ownership gives you rights to the corresponding percentage of the companies risk and rewards. If the company does not perform well, the value of the stock decreases. However, if the company grows, the stock value increases and in some cases shareholders receive cash payments in the form of dividends.

Taxes – portion of income that is owed to federal and state governments. A person or business can reduce their taxable income by spending money on tax deductable expenses. When you budget or forecast revenue, always factor in the impact of taxes on your net income.

Yield – the percentage beyond the original principle that an investment produces. Investment decisions are typically based on expected yield, which should be based upon historical performance.

Personal Reflections

Personal Reflections

About the Author

"Knowledge in youth is wisdom in age." This English proverb aptly describes the heart of this author and the goal of "Guiding Principles for Managing Money." Derek E. Johnson writes this book from lessons learned as a former student and the mindset of a successful businessman. Derek is a graduate of Morehouse College and Georgia Institute of Technology where he earned both a Bachelor of Science in Mathematics and a Bachelor of Electrical Engineering, respectively. He also holds a Master of Business Administration degree from Coles College of Business at Kennesaw State University in Marietta, Georgia.

Derek has worked in various positions ranging from engineering to product managing software. He continues to explore other opportunities to share his talents and passion for empowering those around him. If you had the chance to talk with Derek one-on-one, you would undoubtedly leave with a feeling of hope and inspiration. He has the unique ability to challenge your dreams to help you REALIZE your dreams. Derek's spirit is fueled by the success of others and "Guiding Principles for Managing Money" is an attempt to ensure the reader's financial success.

"Guiding Principles for Managing Money" is the first book in the You Always Have Options^{SM} series.